COMPLETE GUIDE TO
Growing *and* Cultivating
Herbs & Spices

Published 2024—IMM Lifestyle Books, an imprint of Fox Chapel Publishing, 903 Square Street, Mount Joy, PA 17552, *www.FoxChapelPublishing.com*

ISBN 978-1-5048-0136-2

The Cataloging-in-Publication Data is on file with the Library of Congress.

We are always looking for talented authors. To submit an idea, please send a brief inquiry to acquisitions@foxchapelpublishing.com.

Printed in China
10 9 8 7 6 5 4 3 2 1

COMPLETE GUIDE TO
Growing *and* Cultivating
Herbs & Spices

Expert Advice for Planting Indoors and Outdoors, the Best Containers, and Storage

Linda Gray

IMM **lifestyle** books™

Read. Learn. Do What You Love.

Contents

Introduction

Over the past couple of decades, processed sugars and excess salt have infiltrated our diets and changed the way we perceive pleasurable tastes. The increased focus on healthy eating and the popularity of growing your own food has helped promote the idea of exploring new tastes, and is steering the family's taste buds away from sugary snacks to appreciating good food and natural flavors.

Herbs and spices that you grow yourself can do just that. Even if you have never grown a plant before, herbs are a good place to start, whether you have a large garden or just a windowsill. The difference between herbs and spices is simply the part of the plant used. The leaves and flowers of plants are generally regarded as the herbs while the seeds, roots, stigmas, and even bark are considered to be spices.

For thousands of years, herbs have been considered magical plants—humans have used them for millennia as food and medicine. Those who knew what to do with herbs were sometimes treated with suspicion and sometimes, they were revered.

Spices, on the other hand, were shrouded in mystery until recent times—their exotic nature and origins were mythologized by the spice traders over the centuries to keep the prices as high as possible.

In our present information-packed world, we can have it all, and growing herbs and spices at home is one of the most satisfying projects anyone can take on. The wonderful tastes of herbs and spices can encourage even the most jaded palate to enjoy good food again. And the healthier food we eat, the less we want the stuff that's not so good for us.

An organic home garden filled with herbs and vegetables.

Planning an Herb Garden

There's a lot to be said for letting your garden grow wild to provide a mini ecosystem for bees, butterflies, and wildflowers. However, if you actually want to produce crops for you and your family to eat, it's necessary to do a little planning.

How to Begin

Herbs and spices can be grown in different places around the garden; for example, it's always a good idea to have a basil plant growing with your tomatoes every year, but many herbs are perennial and will benefit from having their own space.

A custom-made herb garden can thrive for years with very little maintenance, given the right conditions and a little TLC from time to time. One of the best ways to maintain herbs is to actually pick and use them; it's easy to overlook small herbs, but most will benefit if used regularly.

Herbs and spices are very accommodating plants and many will be happy in containers, so if you're short of outdoor garden space, growing in pots is an ideal alternative. As with any sort of gardening, it's best to first decide what you want to grow and then do a little research to make sure it's feasible in your part of the world—growing mangoes outdoors in a cool, temperate climate is probably a non-starter!

What to Grow

The first step to planning your herb garden is to decide what to grow. Firstly, choose which herbs and spices your family likes to eat. The second consideration is your particular climate and soil, and then the space you have available.

The herbs and spices listed in this book are for culinary use, although most have other uses in preventative medicines and cures for minor ailments.

Aloe vera is a useful herb, especially in the kitchen, as the sap from the leaves can be used to soothe minor burns; it is grown commercially now for its healing properties and is added to many products.

If you use a lot of tomatoes in the kitchen, then basil is a must-have in your herb garden since it enhances the flavor of tomatoes, especially homegrown ones. Basil is an annual herb in moderate climates and needs to be sown every year, but other herbs—such as thyme, sage, and mint—will come up on their own year after year.

Read through the descriptions and growing requirements of the herbs and spices in this book and note the ones that appeal to you and that you think you might like to grow. A little planning goes a long way here, but don't get bogged down in too much detail.

Where to Grow

Deciding where to grow your herbs and spices is the next most important step after choosing your seeds or plants. You might already have some idea from when you researched which herbs to grow—some may need to be grown indoors or in a greenhouse, while others may prefer full sun or partial shade. Always take into consideration the preferred environment for each plant. Some plants will run to seed in hot midday sunshine, but many need some sun during the day.

Preparing the Space

Although it's not essential in most cases, you might check the pH balance of your soil since some plants won't tolerate very acidic soil. Get the balance right and you will produce better crops. Avoid digging over a large patch as soon as the weather allows it. Unless you do a physical day job, the chances are that prolonged digging of heavy soil will result in an aching back and could put you out of garden action for weeks. It can also discourage you from continuing. Take it slowly if you're preparing a large plot—a little digging every day will get the job done and it won't feel so much like a chore.

Some people are put off by the idea of gardening because they have the impression that it's back-breaking work, but this doesn't have to be the case. If you're physically challenged or aren't inclined to get stuck into the digging, employ someone else to do the job for you, which will mean that you have all of the pleasures and not too much hard work! Or create raised beds, which need less maintenance and are easier to reach.

Remove any perennial weeds, large stones, and nonorganic debris from the soil and hoe or rake the soil to a fine consistency before planting young plants or sowing seeds.

Before you begin digging, make sure you have a plan in place that considers soil, sun, and other important factors.

Containers can vary, from ceramic planters to old kitchen items (as long as there is a hole at the bottom for drainage).

Designing

Space permitting, a specially designed herb garden is a delightful addition to any garden. It doesn't have to be large—herbs are very accommodating and many will be happy to grow closely together in a small space. Herbs can be grown along the borders of a flowerbed, in a raised bed, or you could adopt the French potager design idea where vegetables are grown in small beds with herbs fringing the edges. This is a good plan when you grow other crops, since the strong scents of herbs and spices help deter bugs and viruses from fruit and vegetable plants. Otherwise, simply have an herb bed as small or large as your garden can cope with.

CONTAINERS

There are very few herbs that can't be grown in containers. You can find containers in all shapes and sizes and a good garden center will have a variety to suit your particular needs. If you're planning to grow plants in large containers or tubs, consider mobility. It may be worthwhile to invest in a pot mover if the plants need to be moved indoors or into a greenhouse or conservatory during the winter months.

Containers should be moved around from time to time to prevent insects and other wildlife taking up residence in or under the pot. They should always be well-drained and preferably placed on a stand to allow for air circulation and drainage. Never let your containers dry out. With a few rare exceptions, water is essential for the full development of your plants.

Look out for old pots and containers in charity shops or yard sales. A few antique-style pots artfully arranged on a patio planted up with thriving herbs can look spectacular. Plain pots can be painted or glazed and personalized to suit your outdoor décor or to enhance the color scheme in your kitchen.

Dealing with Pests

Herbs and spices are naturally a gardener's friend, since many possess strong scents that deter several bugs, especially tiny but destructive aphids. Carefully position herbs around the garden, even if they're in containers, to shield your vegetables and other crops from pests. Luckily, bees are very attracted to the flowers of herb and spice plants, so if you have a plentiful supply of these, bees will love your garden and help pollinate other crops.

One problem that never seems to go away is the slug and snail population. Given the chance, there are few young plants that slugs won't eat. Protect your young plants in whatever organic way possible—a bowl of beer is said to distract slugs from plants, and crushed eggshells spread around the plants' stems will stop these gastropods for a while. Dry sand spread in a similar way helps for a time, but as soon as it gets wet, slugs take no notice of it at all. You can also get the birds to help! Dig over a patch of ground and walk away, allowing the waiting birds to collect any unearthed slugs and snails or their eggs. If you can do this at the crack of dawn when the birds are hungry, so much the better.

The only downside is that encouraging the birds will also put your seeds at risk. When you start sowing and planting, use wildlife-friendly netting and cover all lines of seeds and young seedlings for a few weeks until plants are growing well.

Pest Control

Grow a couple of garlic plants in the rose bed and always include a few in the vegetable garden to deter aphids. A pot of basil growing on a windowsill will prevent flies from entering the house.

Bumblebees not only collect pollen, but can also detect its nutritional quality, which in turn helps them select the best plants.

Recycle, Reuse, Restore

A trip to the garden center can be expensive, even if you're only stocking up on a few basic seed trays or pots. Before making an expensive trip, have a good look around your home—lots of packaging and containers can be utilized in the garden, and you will be doing your part for the environment, as well as saving some cash.

POTS

Save yogurt and dessert-type plastic pots throughout the year for seed sowing and bringing on seedlings. Wash and dry thoroughly and store in a recycling box until they're needed. Punch holes in the bottom of each pot for drainage. Paper towel cardboard tubes and toilet paper rolls make perfect biodegradable pots. They will need cutting in half or trimming. Squash the tubes together in a tray when sowing seeds and they should last long enough to be planted straight out into the garden or re-potted.

TRAYS

Recent decorating projects may have left you with a couple of paint trays hanging around. Wash and dry well, punch a few holes in the bottom for drainage, and keep these in the recycle box. Ask your friends and neighbors if they have any spare paint trays they don't want.

PLASTIC COVERS

A clear mineral water bottle cut in half can be transformed into two mini greenhouses and will protect individual plants from cold nights. Clear plastic sheeting from packaging should also be saved and can be turned into small makeshift cloches, which are invaluable in early spring.

CUTLERY

Keep a couple of old spoons or forks from the cutlery drawer for the garden. They're ideal tools for tending to small plants in a greenhouse or potting shed. Look out for garden possibilities before you commit anything to the trash. Large clean tin cans and old metal buckets can be

A lot of garden tools don't need to be complicated or expensive, so look around your home for anything you could use before going to the store.

transformed into interesting planters once you've made some drainage holes in the bottom. Old chimney pots, wooden crates, and wine boxes all have garden use potential.

GET THE KIDS INVOLVED

Save lollipop and popsicle sticks, straws, and other paraphernalia for pot markers and seed rows. Getting the kids to collect stuff for a project now will help generate lots of interest in the garden later on.

One Plant, Several Uses

Many plants produce edible herbs as well as spices, so you're able to use the plant to its full capacity. In some cases, plants can also be used as vegetables, making them three times as valuable. The four plants within this chapter are extremely versatile: celery and fennel can be used as a vegetable, a spice, and an herb, while coriander and nasturtiums can be used as an herb and a spice, and all are easy to grow in most climates.

Plant Diversity

Nature provides us with all the nutrients and vitamins our bodies need to be healthy and sometimes, plants we classify as common weeds are actually very worthy plants to grow and eat. Dandelion (Taraxacum officinale), for example, tends to grow as a weed in many habitats around the world and is difficult to get rid of in the vegetable garden. However, it's also a very practical plant and can be used rather than dug up and thrown on the compost heap.

For example, the roots of dandelions can be roasted and used as a caffeine-free coffee substitute. Young dandelion leaves can be added to salads and if too bitter, the leaves can be blanched, much like spinach before eating. The sap from the stem is reputedly an effective cure for warts and verrucae. And last but not least, the flowers can be made into a delicious and healthy jam and also into dandelion wine.

If the simple dandelion can provide us with so many useful products, it's no surprise that many other plants do the same. In this chapter, we look at four plants found in the home garden that will give you at least two products for the price of one.

CELERY (*Apium graveolens*)
(*biennial—although some hybrids may be annual*)

Although we consider it to be a vegetable, celery has been used as an herb for centuries. It was very important in Roman cuisine and was also used medicinally. Celery was developed and cultivated into the vegetable we know today during the seventeenth century in Italy and later became popular in other parts of Europe.

Celery herb grows wild in many parts of Europe, Africa, South America, and North America, but won't develop the blanched stalk unless cultivated. Grown as a vegetable in the kitchen garden, a few leaves can be picked and used in the kitchen for flavoring before the stalks have matured.

Wild celery, *Apium graveolens*, is more resistant to pests and diseases than cultivated varieties.

GROWING ADVICE

Celery will grow well in most moderate climates, but needs to be kept warm while germinating and until the plants are strong enough to be put outside.

Start your seeds by sowing in seed trays full of seed compost. Check on the growing recommendations on the seed packet for your region, but generally, celery seed should be sown in early spring. Although the seed can take three or four weeks to germinate, seedlings tend to be prolific when they do start growing.

The plants will be in the tray for quite some time and the seed should be sown thinly. Make sure the soil is very moist and then carefully pull out a few seedlings, leaving space for the others to grow. Make sure you re-cover any exposed roots of the remaining plants.

The compost must be kept moist at all times, so if you're starting them off in a warm conservatory or heated greenhouse, remember to water them regularly—a light spraying twice a day should be enough. The trays must also be well-drained. Celery won't survive in waterlogged soil.

PLANTING OUT

When the plants get to about 4–6" (10–15 cm) tall, they should be planted out in rows in the garden. Wait until there's no danger of a frost and the soil has warmed up a little before planting out.

One way to grow celery, if you want to cultivate the stalks as well as the leafy tops, is to plant in trenches. Prepare the ground well, removing any perennial weeds and large stones, then add some well-rotted compost to the soil. Make a trench and plant the celery, leaving about 12" (30 cm) between plants. If you're growing for the foliage alone, the plants won't need earthing up later in the year, and planting in a trench isn't necessary. Leave about 6–8" (15–20 cm) between each plant and plant in lines or in the herb garden.

To earth up celery plants, pull the earth gently from the surrounding area to cover the stalks. Use a light rake, but be careful not to damage the plants. Some growers tie the celery stalks together to prevent them drooping and exposing the inner stalks.

Without the need for perfectly blanched celery stalks, the celery herb will grow happily in a well-drained container, as long as it gets regular water and is kept weed-free. Start using the leaves as soon as the plants are growing well.

Celery takes a long time to get going and the plants will last most of the year. Some varieties will carry on producing leaves into the following year before going to seed. Celery won't tolerate a frost, so if you have your plants outside, bring them in as the nights start getting colder. Blanched

Container Growing

Celery will grow readily in containers or large pots. Fill well-drained pots with fresh compost and allow 6–8" (15–20 cm) around each plant. Water your containers well after planting and regularly throughout the summer. Keep your plants in a sunny spot on the patio or balcony. They can be grown indoors as long as they have enough light and water. Before the first frosts, plants should be brought inside if possible and kept in a sunny spot in the house or warm greenhouse. Keep the pots watered and the plants will not only flower the following year, but they may also provide fresh celery leaves throughout the winter months.

Always use caution and be gentle when digging up plants to avoid harming the roots.

Celery Soup

If you have a great crop of celery and want to use some up quickly, try this delicious soup!

Ingredients

- 1 large head of celery, trimmed and sliced
- 1 large onion, finely chopped
- 2 leeks (white parts only), sliced
- 2 tablespoons butter
- 1¾ cups vegetable stock
- 1¼ cups milk (optional)
- ¼ cup heavy cream (optional)
- Seasoning of choice
- Fresh parsley or other preferred herbs

Directions

1. In a large pan, melt the butter and gently cook the celery, onion, and leeks. Cook for about 10 minutes on a low heat to soften, but don't let the vegetables brown.
2. Add the stock and any chopped fresh herbs or dried herbs you may have and bring to a boil.
3. Reduce heat slightly and simmer for about 25 minutes or until vegetables are soft.
4. Either season with salt and pepper and serve immediately or . . .
5. Put soup into a blender and process to a smooth purée.
6. Return to the pan and add milk. Bring to simmering and cook gently for about 10 minutes, stirring from time to time. Season with salt and pepper.
7. Serve hot with a swirl of cream and maybe a couple of celery leaves to garnish.

celery stalks must be harvested before the cold nights arrive.

Always double check on your seed packet for your regional growing recommendations. There are many different varieties of celery available, and some will be more suitable to your needs than others. **Note:** Seed sold for cultivation should never be used medicinally.

HARVESTING AND STORING

Collect seed as it ripens in the autumn and use for flavoring. Leaves can be dried successfully and stored in a jar out of direct light. As with most herbs, the leaf is best used fresh. Celery leaf is stronger in taste than the stalks.

MEDICINAL USES FOR CELERY

Celery is used in Ayurvedic medicine for bronchial problems, including asthma, wind, and as a nerve tonic. Seeds collected when ripe are used to distil into oil and dried into powders.

RECIPE IDEAS

Celery is known for its value in a calorie-controlled diet, but in case you just want to enjoy and ignore the calories, try spreading the inside of a celery stalk with cream cheese or peanut butter. It's delicious!

CORIANDER (*Coriandrum sativum*)
(annual)

Although we think of mint and parsley as being the most common everyday herbs, coriander is perhaps the most widely used throughout the world. The fresh leaves are added to many dishes, adding a unique, spicy flavor, and the pungent seeds are used in pickling or left whole in curries and spicy stews. The seeds are also used in sweet dishes and coriander seed has been traditionally used in breads to aid digestion and improve taste.

Coriander has been used for centuries as a flavoring herb. The Egyptians and ancient Greek physicians used it in many medical preparations. Chinese cultures believed it bestowed immortality and there have been findings of coriander seeds in tombs from over 5,000 years ago.

It is thought to be native to southern Europe and parts of Asia. The Romans spread the word about coriander throughout Europe and it now grows wild in many regions.

GROWING ADVICE

Coriander seed can take a little while to germinate. The seed should be sown *in situ*, as seedlings don't transplant well. Prepare the ground by digging over and removing any perennial weeds and large stones. Rake to a fine consistency and sow the seeds 1½–2" (4 cm) apart in drills about ½" (1 cm) deep.

If you're growing coriander for the seed, you can encourage the plant to seed quickly by planting in a sunny position. The plants grown for foliage would appreciate a little shade during the hottest part of the day. When your plants start producing flowers, pick them off to encourage more leaf growth, or leave them to mature and produce seed.

Sow a short line every few weeks to keep a constant fresh supply, starting in early spring. If there's a frost expected, cover with a cloche overnight. Coriander seed can also be sown by scattering over a prepared bed and gently raked over. Try this if you have plenty of seed to spare when it won't matter too much if the birds get a few or the cat digs them up. Keep plants weed-free and watered well during very hot periods. When the plants are a couple of inches high, they should be thinned to about 8" (20 cm) of growing space per plant.

Coriander seeds are an excellent source of vitamin K, which supports bone and heart health, as well as helping your blood clot to prevent excessive bleeding after a wound.

Coriander, like many herbs, thrives in containers or pots as long as they're well-drained and kept watered. Keep a pot on the windowsill in the kitchen.

Once established, a coriander bed can last for many years. Although an annual plant, it will reseed itself if the temperature doesn't drop too low. Left to get on with it, a coriander patch can scatter itself to all parts of the garden, but it's not an invasive plant like mint. If it's in the way, pull it up and use it in the kitchen. Sow a short line of seed in the vegetable plot and look after it for the first year, and—with a little luck—it will keep coming back every year. Coriander has a strong smell and deters aphids and other pests in the garden.

The seeds are easy to collect. Keep some for cooking and some to plant the following spring. If you use your own seed for planting, sow a lot more than you would with a packet of hybrid seeds, as germination may be more erratic.

Coriander is fairly hardy and the only thing to watch out for is bolting in the hot sun. For harvesting seeds rather than leaves, that won't be a problem, but if you're growing coriander specifically for the foliage, protect from full sun in the middle of the day.

If your plants seem unhealthy, feed with an organic fertilizer every couple of weeks until they

Container Growing

Coriander grows well in pots and containers that are well-drained and filled with fresh compost. As the seedlings don't transplant well, sow a few in each pot and keep one or two plants to grow on, depending on the size of the pot. Seeds can be sown in biodegradable pots and then the whole pot planted in a larger container later. Be careful not to damage roots and water well after planting. Keep pots in a sunny spot, although a little shade is necessary for leaf production. Coriander plants will often thrive on a sunny windowsill. Don't forget to water them.

pick up. Avoid adding any other nutrients as this can affect the taste of the herb.

HARVESTING AND STORING

Coriander seed is used in kitchens all over the world. Wait until the seed is fully mature before storing. Lay a piece of card or cloth around the

Carrot and Coriander Soup

This recipe is a personal favorite of mine.
(Serves 4)

Ingredients
- 1 pound carrots, peeled and sliced
- 1 onion, peeled and chopped
- About 2 pints vegetable stock
- A little cooking oil
- A large bunch of fresh coriander, washed and chopped
- Seasoning (salt and pepper)

Directions
1. In a heavy-bottomed saucepan, heat the oil and cook onions and carrots for a few minutes, stirring so as not to burn. The vegetables need to have started to soften, but not yet browned, about 3 or 4 minutes.
2. Stir in any seasoning you prefer and cook gently for another minute. Stir well.
3. Add the vegetable stock. Bring to a boil and simmer until the vegetables are tender, about 15 minutes.
4. Process in a blender or use a hand blender until smooth.
5. Reheat gently in the pan and stir in the fresh chopped coriander. Serve while hot.

plant when you see the seeds starting to turn brown and then simply collect them as they fall.

The leaves can be dried and stored for many months before they lose flavor. Hang stalks upside down in a dark airy place in paper bags indoors until dry. Crumble and keep in an airtight jar out of direct light. Label.

MEDICINAL USES FOR CORIANDER
Although the Chinese have believed coriander bestowed immortality, it has yet to be proven! It does, however, aid digestion by chewing seeds and adding them to food. The bruised seeds are made into preparations for easing rheumatic pain.

RECIPE IDEAS
Coriander is sometimes known as the curry herb because it adds a mild curry spice taste to your meals. Add fresh chopped coriander to soups, stews, casseroles, and even bread.

A Quick Chicken Curry Cheat
In a large pan, fry diced chicken for a few minutes then add a tin of chopped tomatoes and cook gently until chicken is cooked through, adding a little stock if needed. Then, stir in a handful of chopped fresh coriander and cook for another minute or two. Serve with rice or jacket potato.

FENNEL (*Foeniculum vulgare*)
(biennial, perennial, and sometimes cultivated as an annual)

Fennel is indigenous to Mediterranean areas, but has spread over many parts of the world. The ancient Chinese believed fennel would cure snake bites and the ancient Greeks believed it to be a helpful slimming aid. There seems to be a revival of that opinion in recent years. Fennel certainly aids digestion and helps improve appetite.

In Medieval times, fennel was an herb used to repel witches and has also been used as an insect repellent. It can cause other plants to run to seed or even die back entirely. Fennel works best in its own space. The plants can grow to 7' (2.1 m) tall and cover a large area.

Fennel is a multi-purpose plant. The seeds, leaves, and bulbous root are all edible. It's unlikely that wild or home-cultivated seed will grow into a plant capable of producing a large bulbous root, but it will produce plenty of foliage. Buy hybrid seeds to cultivate the root.

GROWING ADVICE

Fennel is one of the easiest of herbs to grow if you're planning to use the leaves only. Producing a healthy swollen fennel bulb takes a little more practice. The only problem with fennel is that it tends to bolt (run to seed) fairly quickly in the hot sun and sometimes when transplanted.

Give your plants lots of water and keep shaded from the midday sun for a week or two until they get established. Sow seed indoors in early spring. Use bio-degradable pots, if possible, to reduce the risk of root damage when replanting. Fill pots with fresh potting compost, and make sure whichever type of pots you use are well-drained.

Keep warm and watered. Compost should be kept damp, but not wet. When all danger of frost has passed, normally in late spring to early summer, plant out in the garden. Choose a sunny spot at the back of a bed. The plants grow very tall

Several fennel recipes call for the bulb, and because it can be expensive to buy, it's best to grow at home.

Fennel can be grown in pots and containers, but should never be allowed to dry out. When your young plants are coming up, keep watered and weed-free and watch out for caterpillars. Fennel is a great plant to grow where you may be having trouble with white fly in the garden as it repels it. But caterpillars are attracted to it, particularly the caterpillar of the Swallowtail butterfly. Thin out the seedlings to about 12" (30.5 cm) apart and rows about 2' (61 cm) apart.

If you're growing fennel for the vegetable, the bulbs will start to swell later in the year. Make sure your plants get plenty of water during dry periods. Once the bulb is about the size of a tennis ball, they can be earthed up, but you should check the recommendations on your seed packet, as there are many varieties of fennel available. After earthing up, cut down the foliage and allow the bulb to swell. The plant may sprout some new feathery leaves that are usable in late summer salads.

Fennel will tolerate several light frosts once mature and can be left in the ground well into

and will shade lower-growing herbs or flowers. Fennel shouldn't be grown near tomatoes, beans, coriander, or many other plants. It's best grown on its own or perhaps with dill.

Dig over the ground, fairly deep, if you're growing fennel for the root as well as the leaf. Remove any large stones and perennial weeds. Clean the ground of any non-organic debris and rake over until the soil is fine and ready for sowing. Make sure the soil is well-drained and preferably on the light side. Fennel isn't fond of heavy clay soil. If you have heavy soil, a little sharp sand mixed into the soil first will help. You can plant seed directly outside, as long as the nights aren't too cold and there's no possibility of a frost. Sow your seed according to the manufacturer's recommendations on the seed packet.

Container Growing

Fennel can be grown in containers although plants can grow quite tall, so they may need support or to be positioned against a fence or wall. Sow seed directly in well-drained containers or large pots of fresh compost and keep warm and watered. Don't let the soil dry out and shade from the midday sun in very hot periods.

Fennel with Leeks

Fennel bulbs can be cooked as a vegetable. Give it a go and try this recipe with leeks. (Serves 4)

Ingredients
- 4 fennel bulbs
- Juice of half a lemon
- 2 tablespoons olive oil
- 4 leeks, sliced
- 1 bay leaf
- 2 fresh thyme sprigs
- Salt and pepper, to taste
- ¼ pint chicken or vegetable stock

Directions
1. Preheat oven to 350°F (177°C).
2. Prepare the fennel bulbs. Trim and cut in half, then immediately sprinkle the lemon juice over cut parts.
3. Heat the oil in a frying pan and sauté the sliced leeks for 2 minutes to slightly soften them.
4. Add the fennel to the pan, pushing the leeks to the side, and turn for 1–2 minutes to cover in the oil.
5. Tip contents of the pan into an oven-proof casserole dish.
6. Add the bay leaf, thyme, salt, and pepper.
7. Pour the stock over the vegetables and bake in the preheated oven for 1–1¼ hours, turning the fennel a couple of times during cooking.
8. Remove from oven when fennel is cooked through. Remove bay leaf and serve.

the winter, especially if covered with a cloche or fleece. Dig up before very cold weather or prolonged frost.

HARVESTING AND STORING
The feathery leaves are best used fresh, but could be frozen or dried, if necessary. The seeds can be used before they are mature and can be stored for next year's planting and adding to winter dishes and pickles. Pick the whole seed head and dry upside down in a paper bag to collect the seeds as they drop out.

MEDICINAL USES FOR FENNEL
Fennel is useful for aiding digestion and wind problems. It's used successfully as a mouthwash to help treat sore throats and gum disease, and it has also been proven to help in lactation.

RECIPE IDEAS
Fennel herb leaves can be finely chopped and added to many dishes that would benefit from an anise taste. Mix into green salads or potato gratin or stir some fresh fennel into minced pork to make homemade burgers.

NASTURTIUM (*Tropaeolum majus*)
(*perennial, in colder climates an annual*)

Nasturtiums are a trailing vine plant and can be used for excellent ground cover or trained to climb a trellis or fence. There are various hybrids on the market that will be suitable for either ground cover or climbing, although *Tropaeolum majus* is the preferred edible variety. The taste of nasturtiums has been likened to watercress. The leaves of both plants have a peppery taste and are high in vitamin C.

Nasturtium flowers have been used to decorate homes and food for centuries, and they're an excellent addition to a salad bowl. The leaves are used in salads and add a peppery taste to any meal. The seeds can be used instead of more expensive capers and are a good pickling spice. Nasturtiums will reseed if the conditions are right and you may find them coming up all over the garden. They're a wonderful addition to an herb garden.

GROWING ADVICE

There are a number of different nasturtiums available, but to be sure of a good tasting and decorative herb, use the *Tropaeolum majus* variety. This is a hardy variety and will probably reseed itself year after year given the right conditions. Nasturtiums are possibly one of the easiest herbs to grow. Either buy ready-grown plants from a nursery or garden center and set them about 12" (30.5 cm) apart in the ground or slightly closer if grown in containers.

Ready-grown plants have often been started off in a warm greenhouse or polytunnel and should therefore be introduced to an outside growing place slowly. Keep indoors for a day or two or put them out in warm sunshine and bring them in at night. After a few days, depending on the outside temperature, they should be ready for their permanent spot in the garden.

Or start them off with seed. In some areas, you may only ever need to buy one packet of seeds. The plants will reseed and come up year after year. Choose a sunny and well-drained spot. Dig over your soil well and remove any perennial weeds and large stones. Don't dig in any compost or manure if

Nasturtiums are excellent garden protectors, as they produce an airborne chemical that effectively repels several kinds of insects and pests.

you want an abundance of blooms. If the soil is too rich, you will get more leaves than flowers.

Plant your seeds about 8–12" (20–30.5 cm) apart and water. Keep the weeds away and water regularly. Nasturtiums should be kept watered during the whole growing season. When the flowers start arriving, you can ease off a bit, but they should never be allowed to dry out. Although they need a lot of water, the ground must be well-drained and definitely not water-logged. Waterlogged soil will rot the delicate roots very quickly.

Nasturtiums will also grow successfully climbing a trellis or similar structure. Guide the vines as they grow and secure to the structure using loose ties. Pick the leaves and flowers as you need them. The plants will keep producing flowers for many months and the leaves will be available even longer.

Nasturtiums grow well around cucumbers and are a good companion plant. Also, because of their ground coverage and damp soil, they provide good cover for frogs and toads who in turn get rid of a fair number of slugs. So, to help keep slugs off your cucumbers and other squashes, grow

Container Growing

Nasturtiums grow well in containers but do trail and can grow quite large. Allow about 8" (20 cm) between plants or grow in individual pots or containers. Because of their trailing flowers and bright foliage, nasturtiums are an attractive hanging basket plant. Baskets must be well-drained, never allowed to dry out, and positioned in a sunny spot. In ideal conditions, they will produce a wonderful edible display for many months in the year.

Nasturtium Salad

This salad makes a great edible centerpiece for a dinner party or to serve on individual plates.

Ingredients

- 4 boiled eggs, cut lengthwise
- Lettuce leaves
- Cherry tomatoes, halved
- Nasturtium leaves
- Nasturtium flowers
- A small handful of sunflower seeds
- Olive oil

Directions

1. Wash and dry lettuce and nasturtium leaves gently and arrange on a plate or a serving dish.
2. Sprinkle over some of the sunflower seeds.
3. Place boiled egg quarters and flowers over leaves and sprinkle over the rest of the sunflower seeds.
4. Drizzle a little olive oil over the whole dish or use a dressing of your choice.

nasturtiums with them! Because of the dense, low foliage, nasturtiums will also help blanch a crop of leeks if grown around them.

At the end of the season, this versatile plant produces seed which can be left on the plant to drop and reseed itself next year. Or the seed can be collected when ripe and used in the kitchen. Lay an old sheet or card around the plants when they start producing seed so you can collect them as they fall from the plant.

HARVESTING AND STORING

The seed should be stored when fully ripe in sealed glass jars for pickling spice or flavorings in the kitchen. Store in a cool place out of direct light. Keep some seed to sow in the spring in case plants don't come up on their own. The leaves have a high-water content and don't store well, although they will stay fresh in a fridge for a day or two.

MEDICINAL USES FOR NASTURTIUMS

Nasturtium seed has an anti-bacterial property which could aid in treating minor skin eruptions and respiratory problems.

There hasn't been much research in the medicinal properties of leaves and flowers, but the leaves are said to have high levels of vitamin C and could be useful for treating minor skin conditions.

RECIPE IDEAS

The leaves and flowers of the nasturtium plant are edible, and the seeds can be used instead of capers in pickling recipes. The best way to enjoy nasturtium flowers and leaves are fresh and raw in salads. They have a light, peppery taste and add color and texture to your meal.

Herbs

There are many herbs that can be grown at home, although some may need extra care if you live in a cooler climate and are trying to grow plants that like the heat. This chapter outlines some common herbs that can be grown in almost any climate, and with care, all will thrive in the right environment and conditions. One of the most important conditions for herbs is good drainage.

ALOE VERA (*Aloe vera*)
(perennial)

Historical evidence suggests that aloe vera originated in Africa, although it's now grown in many countries. In moderate climates, aloe is often grown as a houseplant and thrives well in containers. It will grow happily in humid conditions as long as the roots aren't in water. The plant will tolerate very high temperatures as well as very cold air temperatures, but low ground temperatures will damage the roots.

The use of aloe vera in medicinal preparations has been recorded for more than two thousand years. The sap from the leaf of the plant is a thick gel and it's this gel that holds all the healing ingredients aloe vera is becoming more and more known for. There's a wide commercial trade in aloe vera and it has cured many minor ailments, as well as some chronic conditions.

The plant is 95% water and is therefore frost tender. It's normally grown indoors as a houseplant. In warmer climates, aloe vera can be grown outside in full sun or very light shade.

GROWING ADVICE

Aloe vera has become very popular in recent years and is available in the form of ready-grown plants from many garden suppliers. Plants should be kept on a sunny windowsill and kept indoors for most of the year. During warm summer months, pots can be put outside during the day. Don't forget to bring them in before the temperature drops.

From Seed

Aloe vera can be grown from seed, although it can take anything from one to six months to germinate. It must be kept warm during this time. It should be started in well-drained trays or pots of warm fresh compost and kept damp. Water gently but regularly.

When the plants are large enough to handle, prick out carefully into individual pots and keep warm. Position in a sunny spot, either in a greenhouse or on a windowsill. If you're planting outside, choose the sunniest spot in the garden away from draughts and frost pockets.

An interesting feature of aloe vera plants is they continue to release oxygen and absorb carbon dioxide at night, which makes them suitable plants to keep in the bedroom.

The stem cuttings from an aloe plant are called "pups" or "offsets." Dividing aloe pups is the best way to get more plants.

Protect with a cloche or other cover during the night until the plant has become established, and during the next cold season. Remember aloe vera is a tropical plant and likes warm humid weather and plenty of sun.

From Offsets

The quickest way to propagate aloe is to take the offsets from the main plant and repot immediately using new compost in a container that can be positioned in the sun. Offsets should be 3–4" (7.6–10 cm) high and removed carefully to minimize damage to the mother plant.

All pots and containers must be very well-drained. Add extra sand or gravel to compost before planting. Water immediately after planting and then let the soil dry out almost completely before watering again. Use the offsets as they become large enough to remove from the plant to produce new plants.

During the summer months, aloe vera should be watered well and then left to dry out completely before watering again. During the winter months, the plant rests and requires very little water. When the soil is completely dry, add a cup or two of water. The plant is a succulent, so it holds a lot of water within the leaves and roots and will rot if watered too much and too often.

Container Growing

Aloe vera thrives in properly drained containers but may need repotting every year. If the soil you're using is a little tired, you may want to feed the plants a couple of times during the spring and summer months. As mentioned above, allow the pots to dry out before watering. If the top couple of inches of soil feels dry, it's time to water. Keep pots or containers in a sunny or bright spot in the house with plenty of airflow. During hot summer months, containers could be placed outside, but don't leave them out on a cold night.

Aloe Vera Juice

The best way to enjoy and get the most benefits from aloe vera is to juice it! This recipe is a refreshing, hydrating, and vitamin-packed start to the day!

1. Prepare by removing outer layer of the leaf or leaves—the outer layer can cause stomach upset.
2. Add coconut water, lemon juice, a small cucumber, and any other fruit juice you prefer, such as pineapple.
3. Whizz it in the juicer or blender and drink straight away.

Repotting

The plant will need repotting every year or so, depending on the size of the pot, how well it grows, and the quality of the original compost. Aloe vera has shallow but wide spreading roots and should be repotted into a container that's wider, but not necessarily deeper, than its current one. Always use fresh compost when repotting and mix in some sand to help with the drainage.

HARVESTING AND STORING

Aloe vera is an evergreen succulent and available for use all year round. The gel inside the leaves can be stored and is widely processed in aloe vera preparations. However, in commercial processing, it's usual to use the whole leaf, as it's more cost effective.

MEDICINAL USES FOR ALOE VERA

The medicinal uses for aloe vera are well-documented and varied. One particular benefit is a treatment for burns: the sap in the leaves can be applied directly to a minor burn, as it aids the body in its healing process and the wound will be relieved. The sap also relieves pain from stinging insects and plants and will soothe sunburn.

RECIPE IDEAS

Aloe vera can be used in many homemade body care products, such as soap and hair treatments, and can be safely consumed.

ANGELICA (*Angelica archangelica*)
(biennial)

Historically, angelica has always had religious associations. During times of plague, it was believed to have arrived from an angel to protect man from diseases, as well as delivering him from evil and providing protection from witchcraft. In the Middle Ages, angelica root was thought to cure a number of medical conditions. The roots and seeds were burned in the home to freshen air. Generally, it was considered to be the most important of all the medicinal herbs.

In Germany, angelica is often carried in processions—the origins of which go back so far that the true meaning behind this tradition has been lost. There seems to be a connection with paganism before Christianity, which implies this herb has always had religious associations.

Angelica originated in northern countries, but has become naturalized in the UK and other parts of Europe. It is now a common garden herb. Although normally classified as a biennial, angelica will keep growing for many years in the right environment.

The plant can cause skin allergies, so care should be taken when handling. Wear protective gloves if you're prone to skin problems or plant allergies.

GROWING ADVICE

Angelica can grow up to two meters high and should be positioned at the back of an herb garden. It's a biennial plant, but if allowed to mature, it will reseed itself in some areas, and in the right conditions, an angelica patch can be productive for many years before the plant needs replacing, if at all.

Some growers prefer to restrict the plant from flowering to strengthen the root structure. This encourages the plant to become perennial rather than biennial.

Angelica is very pest- and disease-resistant and rarely suffers any problems. The most important thing with angelica is to not let it dry out. It enjoys a moist soil, although it must be well-drained. It will also cope with heavy clay soil. Angelica attracts wildlife and will help encourage the right insects to pollinate all your garden plants.

All in all, angelica is a very easy and practical plant to have in the herb garden, but should never be grown in waterlogged ground.

From Seed

Seed should be planted as soon as possible after ripening, normally late August to early September. Seed can be started in the spring, but the germination rate will be slower and possibly lower. Collect seed from an existing plant and sow in well-drained trays or pots of new potting compost. Keep in a cold frame or greenhouse until the following spring.

Trays and pots should be kept away from cold draughts and the soil must be kept damp. If the compost dries out for any length of time before germination, it's unlikely the seed will survive. When the seeds have germinated and the plants are large enough to handle, prick out into individual well-drained pots of new compost, and keep the pots in a greenhouse or conservatory through the winter. Put the individual plants out into the garden in spring or after the last frost, in their permanent position. Angelica grows very tall, up to six feet or two meters, and should be positioned behind lower-growing plants.

Root Cuttings

Angelica can be propagated from pieces of root from a well-established plant. Dig up the plant carefully to avoid damage and replant the pieces as soon as possible after digging up. Spring is probably the best time to do this, although if there's someone local to you who grows angelica, it's worth asking for their advice, as different regions have different growing seasons.

Angelica thrives in a well-drained sunny spot, but is happy to grow in partial shade and will even grow well in light woodland areas. In very hot summers, the midday sun can burn leaves and damage plants, even the sun-loving ones. Water

You can prolong the life of angelica by cutting off the flowers before they seed, or by cutting the plant to ground level every fall.

Candied Angelica

There are several different methods of making candied fruits. Follow your preferred recipe, but here are some helpful tips.

Choose stems that aren't woody—probably best done in late spring/early summer. Cut into 3–4" lengths.

Generally, stems need to be boiled in sugar syrup, cooled, and boiled again a few times before storing. This process is often carried out over a number of days. It's a lengthy procedure, but worth the wait for the delicious results!

in the morning during the summer months to help protect the leaves and roots from drying out and, if possible, cover with a light garden fleece to protect plants from the hottest part of the day.

Note: If you collect herbs from the wild, extra care should be taken, as angelica is very similar in appearance to hemlock, which is highly poisonous.

HARVESTING AND STORING

Harvest angelica stems when they're young and tender for use in the kitchen. Leaves can be dried by tying into small bunches and hanging in an airy, dark place in paper bags to protect from dust or bugs. The stem of angelica is often candied and used in cake decoration.

Container Growing

Angelica is a tall-growing plant and isn't suitable for most containers. The plants can be started in pots, but should be transferred to open ground as soon as they reach 3–4" in height.

Tea can be made from bruised roots, although **the roots are poisonous if eaten fresh**. Seeds don't store well and should be used as soon as possible after harvesting.

MEDICINAL USES FOR ANGELICA

An infusion made from the bruised root of angelica can relieve bronchial symptoms. It's also a useful herb to aid digestive problems, reduce flatulence, and as a general appetite stimulant. Never consume angelica roots raw and fresh.

Because of the plant's high sugar content, it's not considered advisable for diabetics to take in medicinal form.

RECIPE IDEAS

Angelica leaves can be added to fish or salad dishes.

The stem is often candied and used as a cake decoration, but can also be cooked with rhubarb or apples to make a tasty pie or crumble dessert. Angelica can also be added to jams and preserves.

Angelica has an earthy taste and complements dishes with sharp flavors and brings out the sweetness in many recipes.

BASIL (*Ocimum basilicum*)
(annual)

Basil is native to southern Asia and the Middle East, but will grow as an annual plant in most moderate climates. It was introduced to Europe as a culinary herb in the sixteenth century.

Basil has, for many centuries, been considered to be an herb of love and purity, and many myths and legends have been attached to it, from the belief that it will open the gates of heaven to a sprig worn in the hair will attract your loved one.

It's been cultivated for thousands of years and has been used medicinally, as well as in the kitchen for just as long. Basil was believed to cure many different ailments, from coughs and colds to digestive problems. It has also been used cosmetically to add shine to dull hair. Perhaps the most common use of basil today is its addition to tomato dishes and many people refer to it as the tomato herb.

GROWING ADVICE
Because basil is indigenous to warm regions, the plant will not survive cold temperatures. The seed should be started indoors in spring or outside when the ground has warmed up. Position basil plants with peppers and tomato plants and they will enhance each other's growth.

There are a number of different types of basil, and you should choose one that's suited to your region. Most basil types will grow successfully in a moderate climate if kept warm in the early stages of growth. It's possible to keep basil going throughout the winter, but it will need to be indoors or in a warm greenhouse or conservatory.

If you want to try and keep plants going through the winter months, consider growing in a container and then bring it inside when the temperature starts to drop. Generally, plants should be watered less often during the winter months, although in a centrally heated house, the soil may dry out quickly. Keep an eye on your plants and water when necessary.

Start seeds off in trays or pots of seed compost. Make sure the containers are well-drained. Keep warm on a windowsill or in a greenhouse and

keep the soil damp. Basil plants are normally fairly quick to germinate, and you should see most of the plants up within the first couple of weeks of sowing.

Planting Out

When the plants have four or five true leaves (not counting the first two), they're ready to transplant. Pot in individual pots or containers. When the weather and ground has warmed up, plant some straight out into the garden. Choose a sunny spot. Basil likes lots of warmth and will thrive with five hours or more of sunshine every day. Prepare the soil by digging over and raking to a fine consistency. Remove any weeds and large stones.

Basil isn't a heavy feeder and will tolerate fairly poor soil. The plants stay reasonably small and can be dotted about the garden. The heavy scent repels flies and aphids, so one or two plants in all your vegetable beds will help other crops resist bugs and viruses.

Because basil likes to grow in full sun, drying out can be a problem. Make sure you keep the plants watered, but not waterlogged. The soil should always be well-drained. Seed can be planted directly outside, but the weather conditions must be good. Make sure all danger of frost has passed. Protect seeds and seedlings with

Basil is still edible after it flowers, but large, well-established flowers do cause the leaves to lose their flavor and taste a little bitter.

a cloche at night if temperatures are low. When the plants are a few inches high, they will need thinning and repositioning if necessary.

Basil repels insects, so it doesn't tend to suffer with many problem bugs, although young plants should be protected against slug and snail attacks. Spread broken eggshells around the seedlings or use any other organic method to protect against slugs. When the flower heads begin to grow, pinch out the whole branch and the plant will grow more leaves. Use your basil as much as you like. The more you use it, the more it will grow!

HARVESTING AND STORING

Harvest the whole plant, or bring indoors in its container, before the cold weather. Frost or a very cold spell will finish off a basil plant.

Basil is always tastier if used fresh, but can be very successfully stored by freezing or drying. Hang sprigs or small bunches upside down in a dark, warm but airy room until dry. Crumble leaves into a sealable glass jar and label. Freeze whole sprigs quickly on a flat tray, store in the freezer in sealable bags, and label.

Container Growing

Basil grows well in containers and pots. Keep in a sunny or bright spot and don't let the soil dry out. If kept warm and watered, basil will often carry on growing right into the autumn and will stay fresh and green for picking through to midwinter. In warmer climates, basil will be available practically all year round. Keep a pot of basil near an open window or door to deter flies during the summer months.

Tomato and Basil Salad

This is a super simple salad—only three ingredients needed! The quantity of ingredients vary depending on how many servings you're making.

Ingredients

- Tomatoes
- Basil leaves
- Olive oil or dressing, if preferred.

Directions

Simply slice tomatoes and layer in a serving dish with chopped fresh basil leaves. Drizzle olive oil or a salad dressing if preferred, although tomatoes and basil on their own is just as delicious!

Basil Pesto

This is an excellent pantry staple—you won't need (or want!) to buy pesto from the store again!

Ingredients

- 1 cup fresh basil leaves
- 6 tablespoons pine nuts
- 6 tablespoons grated parmesan cheese
- 1 small garlic clove, crushed
- 1 cup olive oil
- Lemon juice, salt, and pepper, to taste

Directions

1. Lightly toast the pine nuts in a dry frying pan.
2. Put nuts, basil, parmesan cheese, and garlic in a food processor or blender and blend for a few seconds.
3. Add olive oil slowly, blending after each addition until creamy.
4. Add lemon juice, salt, and pepper and blend together for a few more seconds.
5. Serve immediately or store in the fridge for up to 48 hours.

MEDICINAL USES FOR BASIL

Basil belongs to the same family of plants as mint and is considered to be a good digestive aid—a small cup of basil tea after a meal is a good idea! Herbalists use it to help cure headaches, constipation, and sickness.

RECIPE IDEAS

Basil is known as the tomato herb, as it enhances the taste of tomatoes perfectly.

BAY (*Laurus nobilis*)
(perennial)

Bay is an evergreen shrub native to Europe and some parts of Asia. Bay trees will grow up to 50' (15.2 m) tall if left to their own devices and have enough space. For domestic gardens, it's usually grown as a garden bush and kept around 6–7' (1.8–2.1 m) in height.

Its botanical name emphasizes the respect once held for this plant. A rough translation is "noble praise." Bay leaves were strung into headdresses and given to the victor as a crown after physical combat. Bay is known to have powerful antiseptic qualities and is one of the most ancient of all aromatic herbs.

It is a woody plant and propagation is normally done by cuttings or layering. It does grow wild in some parts.

GROWING ADVICE

Bay is usually grown from autumn cuttings or layering the branches. To take cuttings, simply prune the bush or tree back in the autumn and replant the cut stems. Use the pieces of stem with a "heel" still on and strip all but three or four leaves. Dip the cut end in an organic hormonal product, if available, to speed up the root growth, although this isn't always necessary. Plant by pushing the cut end into a fresh container of well-drained compost.

Once your cuttings are planted, stand back and let them grow. Water regularly and keep the container inside in a dark spot in the house. High humidity will give good results when propagating bay. A heated greenhouse is ideal, as long as the pot is kept in the dark. Place under a shelf and cover any low windows. Don't use the leaves until the plant has developed roots and been repotted or planted out.

Planting Out

A bay tree, once established and with a little maintenance, will survive for many years. Position the tree well in lots of sun, out of windy spots, and keep well-drained. Dig a large hole for the roots

If growing to use in the kitchen, bay leaves are best when slow-cooked and add a subtle aroma and flavor.

new plant is then safe to cut from the main plant. Replant in a pot or container or in another part of the garden.

From Seed

Bay can also be grown from seed, although germination may be poor. The seeds take a long time to germinate and should be laid on top of moist compost in a container. Put a fine layer of dry compost over the seeds and keep in a dark place.

Check on the seed packet for the recommended time to sow seeds according to your region, although generally seed should be sown in early to late spring.

Once you get the hang of growing bay from seed, there's no reason why you couldn't try collecting your own seed from the plants when they produce their fruits. The fruits aren't edible, but the seeds are reusable. Dry the seeds carefully and plant more than you would if you were using store-bought seed.

GENERAL GROWING TIPS

Bay is a fairly hardy plant and is resistant to disease and pests, but always make sure your bush or tree has good drainage and is protected or brought indoors during cold winters.

to spread into, and mix some compost in with the soil you fill back in. Heel down firmly and water well. Keep it weed free and watered during dry weather, and let it rest during the winter months.

Although an evergreen, bay doesn't like the cold, and in a cold, winter climate, it should be grown in a pot that can be brought indoors for a few months of the year. Start using the leaves from your tree a few days after planting. Only pick what you need.

Layer Propagation

Gently lay a low-growing branch down along the ground next to the plant without damaging either the branch or the mother plant. Peg the branch into the soil using a U-shaped peg and cover with a fine layer of seed or other rich compost. In about a year, roots should be sprouting, and the

Container Growing

Bay is often grown in containers to restrict its roots. The shrubs can be shaped and their roots will tolerate a tight squeeze for some time before they need repotting, possibly up to five years. The main reason why bay plants die in containers is through lack of water. The soil should be moist, never waterlogged. The leaves start to go brown at the edges when the plant needs water, but a regular watering will keep them thriving.

Bouquet Garni

A bouquet garni is simply a bundle of herbs tied together and used to make soups, stews, stocks, and casseroles.

Bay is the most commonly used herb in *bouquet garni*—literally a bouquet of herbs. There are many variations, but the most common herbs in a *bouquet garni* are bay, parsley, and thyme. Collect a bunch of your favorite herbs (but not too many, three to five at most), add a dried bay leaf or two, and tie together to add to casseroles, stews, and any other dish that will benefit from the taste of herbs.

If other herbs are unavailable, a couple of dried bay leaves added to a beef stew will bring out the flavors and turn your mid-week stew into a gourmet dish! Remove leaves before serving.

Keep weed free, especially while the plant is young, and watered enough to keep the soil moist but not wet. One of the main reasons potted bays die is lack of water. The leaves will start to go brown when the plant is lacking in water.

Prune to shape in the spring. If you leave the bay tree to grow without controlling it a little, it will drain important nutrients from your garden and become unruly.

HARVESTING AND STORING

Unless you're cooking for many, only a few leaves are needed every few days or so, and therefore can be used fresh, although many recipes will suggest dried bay leaves as the fresh taste can be overwhelming.

Bay is one of the easiest herbs to store—simply pick the leaves, brush them off, and put them in a jar. Label and store out of direct light. The leaves will start to lose their flavor after about twelve months.

MEDICINAL USES FOR BAY

Bay isn't particularly known for its medicinal qualities, being more of a culinary herb, although it was once used externally as an antiseptic and to help relieve rheumatic pain.

RECIPE IDEAS

Fresh bay leaves can be very strong tasting and most recipes will suggest using dried leaves. Dry fresh leaves and store them out of direct light.

Bay is the chief ingredient in **bouquet garni** *and no self-respecting chef would forget to add bay to soups and stews!*

BLACKBERRY (*Rubus fruticosus*)
(*crown is perennial, stems are biennial*)

The fruit of the bramble plant has been picked and eaten for over two thousand years, but wasn't cultivated in the home garden until very recently. Brambles grow wild in several regions across the world and the thorns prevent the plant being damaged by grazing wildlife. Birds, however, can use thick bramble growth as protection.

Cultivating blackberries is a relatively new idea, as the plant has grown wild for centuries. However, hedgerows and natural habitats have died out over recent years, and it's well worth growing blackberries in your back garden.

New hybrid varieties are a good idea if you want to have blackberries without thorns. These plants are far more practical in a home garden, although any wild variety of blackberry can be trained and kept in order with a little maintenance.

GROWING ADVICE

Blackberries are one of the few fruits that will develop and mature in shade. The plants will produce fruit even in the deepest shade, although the fruits will not be quite as large or grow as quickly as plants that are getting some sunshine.

To produce the best berries, choose a sunny and partial shade position if the space is available in the garden.

Generally, canes (cuttings) are used to propagate the plants.

From Canes

Canes can be bought or obtained from a local grower, and care should be taken when positioning them. Blackberry plants can last for fifteen years, so they will need a permanent patch to thrive and produce healthy leaf and fruits. To take cuttings from an established plant, simply cut the stems after the last fruits have been harvested and replant in a seed bed for the winter until roots have developed. Plant out the following spring. If a long hot summer is expected, it may be better to leave the cuttings until the following autumn before planting out into their final position.

Container Growing

Brambles, or blackberry plants, can grow large and a container should be chosen to allow for growth. There are some smaller hybrid varieties designed for growing in pots and containers, but some will need supporting. Install a trellis for the plant to climb up or put canes in the pots before planting to support them.

Because blackberry plants are hardy and flower quite late in the season, there's never a problem with frost. The ground must be well-drained, but moisture is necessary, so a damp spot in the garden is ideal as long as the ground doesn't become waterlogged. Dig over the planting area in the summer before and incorporate plenty of organic matter, well-rotted compost, etc., as this will help keep the moisture in the ground.

The best time to plant your canes is in the autumn, but if the ground isn't frozen, they can be planted anytime up until the following spring. Allow about 18" (45.5 cm) between plants. It's advisable to check on the growing recommendations that should be supplied with your canes when you buy them. Hybrid varieties can vary in size and space required. Plant firmly and water in. If the ground is damp, canes may not need any more water. Some hybrids may require watering during a dry spring and summer.

Layering

Propagate more plants by layering in September or when the last of the fruits have been harvested. Choose a low-growing, healthy-looking branch from a well-established plant and peg to the ground where it's comfortable and not straining either the branch or the mother plant. Push the branch into the prepared earth about 6" (15 cm) deep and leave until the next spring before digging up to replant. Dig up carefully when roots have developed, then cut the branch between the mother plant and the new one. Replant immediately.

HARVESTING AND STORING

The blackberry fruit is best eaten fresh on the day that it's picked, although they will keep in a fridge for three or four days. Blackberries can be frozen, but lose some of their texture and taste. Cooking the fruit in a pie, for example, before freezing will

Blackberry and Apple Crumble

This is a delicious dessert for anyone who enjoys a classic, fruity crumble pie.

Ingredients

- 2 large cooking apples or 3–4 dessert apples
- Enough blackberries to fill about a third of an oven-proof dish
- A little sugar

Crumble Mixture:

- ½–¾ cup flour
- 4 tablespoons hard butter, cut into small cubes
- 4 tablespoons sugar

Directions

1. Preheat oven to 350°F (177°C).
2. Peel and core apples and cut into thin slices. Put into a pan with a little water.
3. Bring gently to a boil, then reduce heat and simmer lightly until apples are tender.
4. Drain apples, reserving the liquid.
5. Lay apple slices in an oven-proof dish and top with enough prepared blackberries to fill the dish to half or two-thirds full.
6. Sprinkle a little sugar over the fruit and then pour over a couple of tablespoons of the reserved liquid or use water.
7. Make crumble mix by rubbing butter into the flour until mixture resembles breadcrumbs, adding a little more flour if too sticky. Stir in the sugar and pile the mixture on top of the fruit. Smooth out gently with a knife or back of a spoon.
8. Bake in the center of a preheated oven for about half an hour, or until the top is starting to turn golden brown. Don't overcook.
9. Serve hot or cold with custard or cream.

Note: If you don't have any apples, use blackberries on their own. You may find that an extra spoonful of sugar is needed to sweeten the fruit. Sometimes blackberries can be a little sharp.

Blackberry plants make for an excellent trellis-growing fruit to have in the garden.

help camouflage the poorer taste or texture. A juice can be made from the fruits and stored in sealed jars or frozen in ice cube trays.

The young leaves can be dried. Hang in small bunches until crisp enough to crumble. Store in glass jars and label.

MEDICINAL USES FOR BLACKBERRY

Blackberries have been used to aid digestion, help reduce symptoms of colds and fevers, and as a general tonic since earliest times. A tea made from young leaves is high in vitamins and acts as a tonic to the system. The fresh fruits are packed with fiber and vitamins and should be incorporated into the diet whenever possible.

RECIPE IDEAS

Blackberry leaf tea helps strengthen the immune system. Put young fresh leaves into a jug and pour over boiling water. Leave to steep for 3–5 minutes.

The leaves and fruit of the bramble are both high in vitamin C, as well as being delicious. The leaves can be used to make teas to aid in recovery from many minor ailments.

BORAGE (*Borago officinalis*)
(annual or sometimes biennial)

Borage was always believed to be the herb of courage and was given to soldiers before going into battle. The herb also bestows a general good feeling and is often added to alcoholic drinks and summer punches. It has been used for centuries as an herb to make you feel happy and is said to alleviate depression.

In Roman times, much was recorded about borage and right through to the Middle Ages, the flowers were added to salads. The leaves and flowers were used in cordials. In recent years, borage hasn't been so widely used, but it's a wonderful plant to have available.

It's an annual herb, although it can sometimes be biennial, growing about 3–4' (0.9–1.2 m) tall. Borage produces beautiful star shaped bright blue flowers that attract bees and other wildlife and look beautiful in the herb garden.

GROWING ADVICE

Generally, being an annual plant, borage is usually grown from seed, although the roots can be divided or cuttings can be taken. It's a hardy plant and will reseed itself and take over the garden if not checked. Borage likes full sun, but will grow happily in part shade.

If the weather is warm enough, borage will tolerate very poor soil and dry conditions, but ideally the soil should be fairly rich and damp to produce bigger healthier plants. Borage can grow up to 3–4' (0.9–1.2 m) in height, so should be positioned at the back of a bed to avoid overshadowing lower-growing plants.

From Seed

Dig over a well-drained area of ground in early spring and incorporate lots of well-rotted manure or compost. Remove any perennial weeds and nonorganic debris. Borage seed can be sown in late spring directly outside or later in the year. Check your seed packet for growing recommendations for your area. Annual plants can be sown as early in the spring as possible after all danger of frost has passed, or the seeds are

protected with a cloche. Warm up the soil a little with a cloche for a few days before sowing.

Rake over the area to a fine consistency and then scatter seed sparsely. Cover the seed with a thin layer of soil and water using a watering can with a rosette to avoid washing the seed away. The seed can also be sown in shallow drills in fine soil.

Keep the area weed-free and thin out the seedlings when they're large enough to handle. Allow about 15" (38 cm) between plants. Pull out the weaker plants when the soil is damp to avoid damage to the remaining plants. Water first if necessary. Borage doesn't transplant well, so it should always be sown *in situ*.

Root Division or Cuttings

Root division or cuttings should be taken in early spring or late summer and replanted as soon as possible. Place 3–4" (7.5–10 cm) cuttings in their permanent position and protect from extreme temperatures during the winter. Root division isn't generally as successful because borage is

When in flower, borage is a spectacular plant and shouldn't be hidden away in the garden.

predominantly an annual plant, although, in the right conditions, it can self-seed.

A borage patch can easily become invasive and should be checked regularly for takeover bids on your other herbs. Borage likes a rich damp soil and should be watered regularly in dry periods. A semi-shady spot in the garden will keep the moisture in the ground longer, and borage will thrive there if it gets some sun every day.

HARVESTING AND STORING

Borage leaves and flowers are best used fresh, but can be dried. Hang sprigs of leaves in small bunches inside paper bags to avoid dust in a dark airy place, then crumble and store in a sealed jar. Label and store out of direct light. Leaves can also be dried using a home dryer or very slowly in the oven. Leave the door ajar and turn from time to time. Spread flowers on a heatproof tray and dry very slowly on a low oven temperature or in a home dryer.

Container Growing

Borage plants grow large, and their container should be at least 12" (30.5 cm) in diameter and deep enough to contain a long tap root. Seed can be sown directly into the pot, but a 12" pot will only accommodate one plant. Pots must be well-drained and preferably placed in a sunny spot outside. Water regularly, especially when the weather is dry and sunny.

Borage Syrup

Although this recipe takes a while, it's worth the wait! Note that I've used cups, as it requires measuring rather than weighing.

Ingredients
- About 2 cups fresh borage flowers
- Sugar (see recipe, quantity may vary)
- Boiling water

Directions
1. Pour boiling water over 1 cup of flowers in a bowl and leave overnight to steep.
2. Strain the liquid into a pan and bring to a boil.
3. Pour this liquid over the other cup of flowers in a bowl and again leave overnight or for at least 8 hours.
4. Strain the liquid, pressing all the juice through the strainer with a wooden spoon.
5. Measure how much liquid you have; add to the pan with a cupful of sugar to every 1¼ cups of water. Stir well.
6. Heat gently until the sugar has dissolved, stirring all the time with a wooden spoon.
7. Bring to a boil and boil until mixture thickens. Skim and pour into prepared warm sterilized jars. Cool and store in the fridge.

MEDICINAL USES FOR BORAGE

Borage has anti-inflammatory properties and is often used in treating colds and chest complaints. Natural healers use it in remedies for balancing metabolism and to alleviate menopausal symptoms. It's also the herb of courage and is added to alcoholic drinks and cordials to encourage good feelings.

RECIPE IDEAS

The flowers are most often used in decorating sweet dishes, such as celebration cakes, and the young leaves are used in salads.

The stem and larger leaves can be cooked as a vegetable. The leaves have a slight cucumber taste, making it a refreshing herb to have in the herb garden.

Young leaves can be added to salads and larger leaves can be steamed or wilted like spinach.

Flowers can be made into syrups and candied for cake decorations.

Add borage flowers to any dessert as a garnish to add color and playful charm!

BURDOCK (*Arctium lappa*)
(biennial)

Burdock is one of the plants you may often come home from a walk with, although you may not realize it until you take your outer garments off. It has sticky burrs, the fruit of the plant, which stick to clothes readily. Burdock was, apparently, the original inspiration for the invention of VELCRO®.

The herb is prolific in the wild and is rarely grown in the home garden. It will self-seed and take over if not checked. However, burdock is a useful herb to grow. It's a large and somewhat unruly plant, but can be cultivated and kept under control in a herb garden.

Burdock is traditionally a medicinal herb and has been used throughout the centuries for any number of conditions, from hair loss to digestive problems. The ancient Greeks were one of the first to record its attributes and it's still used today by modern herbalists.

Note: If collecting roots from the wild, extra care must be taken as the roots of Deadly Nightshade are very similar to burdock.

GROWING ADVICE

Burdock grows freely in the wild, but if you choose to cultivate it at home, it can be started from seed in the spring or autumn.

Burdock prefers a full sun position, but will tolerate part shade. Generally, plants grow up to 4' (1.2 m) tall and should be positioned at the back of a bed to avoid lower-growing plants being overshadowed. Some varieties are even taller. Dig over the ground deeply. Burdock is predominantly a root crop, and the ground should be as clean as possible up to about 2' (61 cm) in depth. Remove all perennial weeds, nonorganic debris, and large stones. Dig in some well-rotted manure or compost in the season before planting. Burdock likes a fairly rich soil, but any un-rotted material will cause deformation of the root crop.

In the spring, rake over the ground to a fine consistency and sow burdock seed about half inch (1–2 cm) deep in lines about 2' (61 cm) apart. For autumn sowings, seed should be sown slightly

deeper. Check on your seed packet for growing recommendations in your area. Tamp down the soil with the back of a rake or trowel over the lines of seed. Water well. When your plants are about 6" (15 cm) high, thin to allow about 6" (15 cm) of growing space between them. Do this when the ground is damp or wet so the seedlings can be removed easily without disturbing the others. Pull out the weaker plants.

If you're growing burdock for the root crop only, leaves should be pruned regularly to encourage the plant to strengthen and produce larger roots. Young leaves can be used as a green vegetable and can be picked as soon as the plant is thriving.

Pick off flowers as they appear to promote growth. One or two plants could be allowed to flower for the seed. Burdock usually flowers in late summer and fruits in the autumn. The fruit is the "burr," which houses the seed. The roots take more than three months to mature, and some burdock varieties will take longer. There are hybrids available that will produce roots up to 4' (1.2 m) in length.

HARVESTING AND STORING

Dig up spring sown plants in the autumn, or when the roots are 1–2' (30.5–61 cm) long. Use a fork and ease the soil away from the plant gently so as to not damage the root. Do this when the soil is damp or wet.

Collect the burrs when they're dry and stick to your clothes. Shake out the seeds for storing. Roots can be stored in a fridge for about a week and they can be thinly sliced and dried.

Container Growing

Burdock can grow up to 9' (2.7 m) tall and—because of its height and large roots—it's not generally considered to be a herb that adapts well to growing in pots and containers.

Young leaves can be dried and should be laid out in the sun until crisp. Crumble and store in sealed jars, out of direct light. Label.

MEDICINAL USES FOR BURDOCK

The roots, leaves, and seed are used widely in medicinal preparations for many varied conditions.

Burdock is known to be an effective treatment for skin conditions, as well as being helpful in reducing symptoms of menopause.

Generally, the root is used in tinctures and poultices. The bruised leaves can soothe swellings and bruises.

RECIPE IDEAS

Burdock root often appears in Japanese recipes and can be treated as other root vegetables. It can be shredded and braised or roasted.

Dandelion and burdock has been a popular, commercially made drink for many years and is made from fermented dandelions and the root of the burdock plant.

Burdock root contains prebiotics, a natural dietary fiber, and more antioxidants than common fruits and vegetables.

CHAMOMILE (*Chamaemelum*)
(perennial)

Two main types of chamomile are widely grown; Roman Chamomile (*Chamaemelum nobile*) and German chamomile (*Matricaria recutita*). Both have similar qualities and are used in similar ways. Records show that the Egyptians worshipped chamomile and used it in medicinal aids, as well as cosmetic preparations. It has been used for centuries all over Europe and was distributed further during the sixteenth century.

Its daisy-like flowers make it an attractive addition to an herb garden and, as the plant is perennial, it will grace your garden for many years. Chamomile often grows around the edge of gardens and can be found in the wild. The plant reseeds itself readily, but is easily controlled. It's often left to grow between paving slabs and alongside pathways. When walked on, the plant releases a pleasant scent.

GROWING ADVICE

Small plants are sometimes available at garden suppliers, but chamomile is easily propagated from seed which normally germinates fairly quickly. Chamomile can grow up to a meter in height but generally it will grow as a shrub around 2–3' (61–91 cm) high. Hybrid varieties may differ slightly. It makes a good edging plant especially around a lawn or grassed area.

From Seed

Once established in your garden. Chamomile rarely needs resowing. In the right conditions, it will readily reseed itself and come up year after year. It can also be grown successfully in pots which should be well-drained, but never allowed to dry out. After a couple of years in the same pot, feed with an organic fertilizer or transplant to a bigger pot with fresh compost.

When the plant is in full bloom, chamomile is a perfect container plant to enjoy around a seating area in the garden. Roman chamomile tends to stay as a low growing plant, often only growing to about 12" (30.5 cm) high. Check on the seed packet before you buy so you're sure which variety

While only the flowers are used in the home, the whole herb is used in commercial beer making.

Chamomile can be ready within eight to nine weeks, from seed to harvest—fairly quickly!

you're growing. German chamomile grows much taller and will need to be positioned at the back of a bed to avoid overshadowing low-growing plants.

Choose a sunny, well-drained spot in the garden. As soon as the ground is workable in the spring, dig over and remove any perennial weeds and nonorganic debris. If the ground has been worked a lot or not at all, dig in some well-rotted compost or organic fertilizer. Rake the ground to a fine consistency.

Seeds can be scattered over the prepared area and carefully covered with a light layer of soil. Or sow the seed in very shallow drills. Water gently with a spray or rosette attachment on a watering can to avoid disturbing the seed. Keep the area free of weeds and the soil damp, but not waterlogged. When the seedlings are large enough to handle, thin them to about 12" (30.5 cm) apart,

when the soil is damp. Again, though, check your seed packet for growing recommendations. Some varieties will need more space.

When the new plants come up around your main plant in the following year, as they no doubt will, remove them gently and try replanting them. Water well directly after planting. Or replant into pots of fresh new compost. Keep in a sunny spot, but don't allow the pots or containers to dry out.

If you'd rather not scatter the seeds, sow in biodegradable pots. Keep the seedlings protected from cold and water regularly. When the plants are large enough to plant out in the garden and all danger of frost has passed, plant the whole pot and water well. The pot will degrade in the soil and won't damage the roots of your plants.

HARVESTING AND STORING

The flowers can be harvested as soon as they're in full bloom and added to salads or used in tisanes. Pick flowers gently and fairly regularly and the chamomile plant will produce more blooms throughout the season.

Chamomile flowers can be dried and stored for several months. Pick when the flowers are in full

Container Growing

Chamomile is well-suited to containers and pots. Pots should be at least 8" (20 cm) in diameter. Sow seeds and remove weaker seedlings as they grow, keeping one or two plants to grow on. Pots must be well-drained but watered regularly so the soil doesn't dry out.

Chamomile Salad Dressing

Add a relaxing taste to your salads using chamomile flowers. Sprinkle a few flowers into a green salad to add taste and texture.

Ingredients
- 2 tablespoons fresh chamomile flowers
- 2 tablespoons olive oil
- 1 tablespoon honey
- Juice of 1 lime or lemon, or 1 tablespoon apple cider vinegar
- Salt and pepper, to taste

Directions
1. Mix all ingredients together in a food mixer or use a hand whisk, mix honey and juice or vinegar together first.
2. Whisk in the olive oil and stir in the chamomile flowers.
3. Taste and season as required. Use immediately or store in a sealed jar for a day or two. Whisk again before serving.

bloom and lay on trays to dry in the sun or in a very slow oven with the door ajar.

Sprigs can also be hung in small bunches in paper bags to collect flowers as they dry. When the flowers are completely dry, store in a sealed glass jar and keep out of direct light.

MEDICINAL USES FOR CHAMOMILE
Chamomile has mild sedative properties and has, for many years, been made into a soothing and calming tea. It aids digestion and alleviates symptoms of the common cold. Chamomile is used in cosmetic preparations, including hair lighteners and shampoos. It has also been found useful for reducing joint inflammation, such as arthritis, and easing menstrual cramps.

RECIPE IDEAS
Chamomile is probably best known for its calming properties and is therefore an excellent ingredient for tea. Steep chamomile flowers in boiled hot water for about 5 minutes. Strain and drink when cool enough. Stir in a little honey to taste.

CHERVIL (*Anthriscus cerefolium*)
(annual)

Chervil is in the same family as carrots and is similar to parsley. There are two main varieties—one with flat and one with curly leaves. It has a taste a little like anise and brings out the flavor of other herbs when cooked together.

It was once known as *myrris* because of its resemblance to myrrh. It has been used in religious ceremonies and also has many medicinal qualities. In Roman times, chervil was used as a spring tonic, but it isn't widely used as a medicinal herb these days. It's mostly used in the kitchen and is one of the main herbs in French cuisine as part of the *fines herbes* mixture. The other herbs—chives, tarragon, and parsley—complement each other and chervil brings out the taste in all of them.

Chervil is native to Middle Eastern countries, but can be grown easily in many moderate climates.

GROWING ADVICE
Chervil can run to seed very quickly, especially in hot sun, and should be positioned in a partly shady spot in your garden. Chervil doesn't transplant well and should be started from seed *in situ*. Dig over the soil in early spring, or as soon as the ground is workable. Make sure the area is well-drained and gets some shade during the day. Remove any perennial weeds and nonorganic debris and rake the soil to a fine consistency. Sow the seed in drills about 1" (2–3 cm) deep and cover gently with soil or compost. Water well. Check on the growing recommendations on your seed packet, but generally the first sowing of chervil can be made in mid-spring.

As the plant is notorious for bolting (running to seed), sow a short line of seed every couple of weeks through to midsummer and then another

Chervil has been used extensively in folk medicine throughout the ages. It was once said that eating a whole plant cured hiccups.

later sowing in late summer for autumn use. In this way, fresh chervil will be available throughout the summer and autumn months. Keep the young seedlings free from weeds and water in dry weather. Chervil won't transplant easily, but will need thinning. To avoid having to throw away too many plants, sow seed as sparsely as possible at each sowing.

Thin plants when they're about 2" (5 cm) tall and the soil is damp. Water the area first if necessary. Leave the strongest plants to grow and pull out the weaker ones. Allow about 3" (7.5 cm) of growing space between them. Thin again to about 12" (30.5 cm) apart a few weeks later, again removing the weaker plants. As long as the soil isn't allowed to dry out and chervil doesn't get too much direct hot midday sun, the plants will need little looking after. The hardest thing to control with chervil is running to seed. Avoid direct sunlight and water regularly to alleviate the

While chervil is a short-lived herb, it thrives in a cool, shady area where other plants fail to grow.

problem as much as possible. Pick leaves regularly and cut off flowering stems before they bloom to encourage more foliage.

HARVESTING AND STORING

Harvest leaves as required. Fresh chervil leaves will store well in a sealed bag in a fridge for up to a week. Leaves can be dried and should be hung in a dark, airy place, preferably in a brown paper bag to avoid dust settling. The leaves can also be dried on racks in the sun. When completely dry, crumble and store in a sealed glass jar. Label and store out of direct light.

MEDICINAL USES FOR CHERVIL

The herb is warm and soothing and is often used as a digestive aid in the form of a tisane. A cold infusion of chervil tea is a soothing eyewash.

Container Growing

As chervil likes part shade, it's ideal for growing indoors in pots on a windowsill. Use well-drained pots of new compost and sow a few seeds in each pot. Keep the compost damp. Remove the weaker seedlings when the plants are about 2" (5 cm) tall and leave the strongest plant to grow. Make sure the pots don't dry out and protect them from direct sun through glass. A north-facing windowsill is probably the ideal spot in your home for chervil.

Herbs 53

Frankfurt's Green Sauce

Frankfurt's Green Sauce is a traditional recipe from Germany. Every family will probably have its own version, but basically, it's an herb sauce served cold over boiled eggs and boiled potatoes.

Ingredients

- ½–¾ cup mixed fresh herbs—traditionally 7 herbs; chervil, borage, cress, parsley, burnet, sorrel, and chives
- ½–¾ cup crème fraiche or sour cream
- ½–¾ cup full fat yogurt
- 1 small onion
- 1 teaspoon mustard
- 1 tablespoon olive oil
- 1 tablespoon lemon juice
- Salt and pepper, to taste

Directions

1. Wash the herbs and remove the leaves from stems and roughly chop. Place in a deep bowl.
2. Add the yogurt and crème fraiche or sour cream to the herbs. Purée the herbs with a hand blender (or finely chop them and mix with the yogurt mixture).
3. Chop onion very finely and add to the mixture with the rest of the ingredients.
4. Rest for an hour in the fridge or a cool place before serving.
5. Serve with hard-boiled eggs and/or boiled potatoes for a tasty mid-week treat.

Young, tender leaves added to salads not only improve the flavor of your meal, but are also believed to act as a mild tonic.

RECIPE IDEAS

Chervil really is a great herb to flavor many meals. Add to soups, risottos, stews, and casseroles, sprinkle a fresh salad with a few chopped chervil leaves, or garnish any dish with whole leaves.

CHIVES (*Allium schoenoprasum*)
(perennial)

Chives are a member of the onion group and grow wild in many parts of Europe and North America, although they originate from China. They have been collected from the wild for centuries, but weren't cultivated until the Middle Ages. There are a number of different hybrids available including a "garlic" variety.

Chives are easy to grow and produce purple or white edible flowers that can be used to garnish a meal, or dried and used in a flower arrangement. The bright green leaves are used in the kitchen and their delicate onion flavor enhances any meal. And they also decorate a kitchen windowsill nicely!

In a moderate climate, chives will die off in the fall and then reappear the following spring.

GROWING ADVICE

Chives are perhaps one of the easiest herbs to grow. They can be grown in pots outside or indoors on a windowsill and they like to be used, so remember to cut them regularly. Placed in odd corners of the vegetable garden, they will help deter pests from your crops. Allow them to spread and they will take over a whole patch of your herb garden.

Chive plants make an impressive border around an herb or vegetable plot. The one place you don't want to grow chives, however, is near onions. The onion fly is one of the few bugs that attack chives. They're a beautiful display plant, usually with purple or white flowers, and always look fresh and green, as well as being edible.

From Seed

Chives are one of the few plants in the onion family that are easy to grow from seed. They tend to germinate well and fairly quickly. Prepare a well-drained seed tray with seed compost and lightly sow the seed on the surface. Sprinkle a fine layer of compost over the seeds and water using a mister or fine spray. Keep the compost damp and the seed tray in a warm place.

Let the seedlings develop a little before planting out into pots or in the garden. It's a good idea to plant the small plants in pots for the first year and put some out in the garden the following spring or summer. But as long as the baby plants are strong enough, they can be planted directly outside in a warm, sunny spot. Plant out in the evening to allow them to settle in before the midday sun the next day. Water in well especially if a sunny day is expected.

Chives prefer a sunny spot but like a little shade when it gets hot. The soil must be well-drained and all you really need to do is water them occasionally. For outside planting, mix some potting compost in with the soil you're planting into. If you're growing the plants in pots or containers, use fresh potting compost and keep damp but not wet.

Root Division

In the autumn, the plant can be divided, providing it's healthy and growing well. Gently fork up the whole plant taking care not to damage the roots, then carefully but firmly separate the clump of root into two or more pieces. Plant each piece out immediately and water. If you're growing chives in a container, dip the whole pot in water before removing the plant. This will help protect the roots from breaking.

Dunk the whole pot in water and let it drain.

Container Growing

Chives are perfect herbs for containers and can be grown on a bright windowsill indoors. Plants will often stay green and usable right through the winter. Otherwise, they can be planted in large pots or containers and placed in a sunny spot on the patio or balcony or scattered around the garden. Their purple or white flowers create a wonderful display for weeks. If their location gets very hot, it may be best to shade chives a little from the midday sun. Always make sure pots or containers are watered regularly and that they're well-draining. When the plants get too big for the pots, separate by root division and repot immediately.

GENERAL GROWING TIPS

Choose a sunny position, although a little shade is preferable in high summer. The soil must be well-drained. Chives won't thrive in waterlogged soil. Chives will tolerate some drought, but will eventually need water. They won't need feeding unless your soil is particularly poor. If it is, then use an organic feed every few weeks.

Chives tend to stay fresh and green throughout the year, but if your plants die back, don't worry, the roots are probably fine and will produce fresh green leaves again in the following spring. When the plant has finished flowering, cut the whole thing down to a couple of inches high and it will start producing fresh green chives again.

HARVESTING AND STORING

Harvest by cutting with scissors from the outside of the plant. Cut down to about 2" (5 cm). Chives can stay leafy all year round in a warm climate so it's hardly worth storing them, but in cold weather,

Potato Salad

Potato salads are a classic crowd-pleaser, but this one made with homegrown chives is extra special!

Ingredients

- 2 pounds new potatoes, scrubbed (or peeled)
- A small bunch of chives, finely chopped
- A handful of chopped walnuts, if available
- ¼–½ cup natural yogurt
- ¼–½ cup mayonnaise
- Salt and pepper, to taste

Directions

1. Steam potatoes until just cooked, but not mushy. Drain well and leave to cool completely.
2. Make sauce by blending mayonnaise and yogurt.
3. When potatoes are cool, cut them into bite-sized pieces and put into a large serving bowl.
4. Mix in chives and walnuts and carefully stir in the sauce, coating all ingredients.
5. Chill for 30 minutes before serving.

Note: Try using crème fraiche instead of mayonnaise or any other preferred dressing. Taste before adding to the potatoes.

they will die back. If yours are prone to do so, freeze a few bunches at the end of the summer.

The flowers can be dried by hanging flower stems upside down in paper bags to avoid dust. Carefully put dried flowers in glass jars, label, and store in a cool, dark place. The leaves are unlikely to dry successfully.

MEDICINAL USES FOR CHIVES

Chives are primarily a culinary herb, but being part of the onion family, they do aid digestion and have also been used in fighting cold and flu symptoms, although onions are probably more effective.

RECIPE IDEAS

Chives have a mild onion flavor and can be chopped and added to many dishes. It's best to add them in last minute or so at the end of cooking. Wash and chop finely. It's sometimes easier to use kitchen scissors to chop chives.

Add to:

- Potato salads
- Hot mashed potatoes
- Omelets
- Stir frys
- Creamy cheese dips
- Risottos
- Salads
- And any other dish that would benefit from a mild onion taste.

COMFREY (*Symphytum officinale*)
(perennial)

Although it isn't advisable to medicate yourself with comfrey, it has been used to treat many medical conditions for generations and is still respected in parts of Europe as a healing herb. It is commonly known as "knitbone" and a poultice of crushed comfrey root is considered to be helpful in relieving injuries, such as broken bones. Comfrey is still widely used in the pharmaceutical industry for treating varicose veins and similar conditions.

The comfrey plant is very high in protein—around thirty-three percent of the plant is pure protein, which is probably responsible for its healing powers. Comfrey tea has been considered an aid in healing many internal injuries, although recent research is pointing to the fact that comfrey can be detrimental to liver function. It is **not advised to take internally.**

Comfrey is often grown as a "green" manure crop. Comfrey is a useful tonic for the soil and helps release the nutrients for your plants to absorb. It's grown as an animal feed crop in some parts of the world. Comfrey is a hardy perennial and will produce leaf for many years in the right conditions and will often crop up to three times every year.

GROWING ADVICE
Comfrey is generally grown by crown division, root cuttings, and transplants. These methods can all be performed during the summer right up until early autumn.

Crown Division
Gently dig up an established plant and pull the crown apart. Replant these pieces as soon as possible after digging up. Comfrey is a hardy plant, so pieces should be okay if left for a day or two. The soil must be well-drained and fairly

Comfrey is often grown as a "green" crop.

light. The comfrey plant is a deep-rooted herb and needs depth of soil to thrive. It won't do well in shallow soil. Comfrey likes some sun, but will still grow well in part shade. It's a good plant to fill up a shady spot in the garden, although it can be invasive as the plants get larger and larger every year. Replant the pieces of crown and water well. Comfrey thrives in a damp soil, but not waterlogged. Plants tend to be fairly self-sufficient and have deep roots, so they will find water where shallow-rooted plants may not. But a watering when the ground is very dry or if the plants are in a particularly sunny spot will help it grow and produce more leaf. Comfrey is one of the fastest growing herbs and within a few weeks, it will have produced leaves up to about 12" (30.5 cm) long.

Root Cuttings

Again, choose a well-established plant. Dig up carefully and break the root apart. Replant the pieces as soon as possible after digging up. Keep the weeds away for the first year while the plants become established, and then watch that it doesn't take over the whole garden! Comfrey is the best herb to use as a tonic for the soil in your garden, as well as an animal feed. Chickens, rabbits, and other animals will happily eat comfrey leaves, although they should be picked a day in advance. This allows the leaves to wilt a little and lose the leaf "hairs." Domestic animals will rarely eat fresh comfrey leaves.

Cut down all the leaves before the plant flowers and use as a tonic for the soil in your garden. Lay fresh leaves in the bottom of trenches dug for potatoes. The comfrey leaves release nutrients into the soil which the potato plants will take up. Comfrey really can help to increase the quality and quantity of your crops.

Or to make a liquid tonic, place comfrey leaves in a tub or barrel with a heavy weight to press them down. Cover for a few weeks. The resulting liquid can be used to feed tomatoes and other summer fruits and vegetables. The only problem with this is that when you lift the cover off, the smell is something like an open sewer. But it's great for the garden!

Container Growing

Comfrey is a deep rooting herb and isn't generally grown in containers. Plants may grow in a deep container, but it must be well-drained and never allowed to dry out. Plants grown outside tend to find their water source via deep roots, but in a pot, they are restricted and will need regular watering.

Comfrey is a very hardy plant and will stick around for years. In very harsh winters, a mulch could be used to protect the roots from freezing, but normally the plants are strong enough to cope with fairly low temperatures.

HARVESTING AND STORING

Comfrey leaves can be harvested up to three times a year, making it probably one of the most prolific herbs in the garden and doesn't tend to need a lot of storing. The leaves can be dried and stored to make comfrey tea during the winter months, although comfrey should never be taken in large doses. Hang the leaves in a dust-free, dark, and airy place until crisp, then crumble into glass jars, label, and store out of direct light.

MEDICINAL USES FOR COMFREY

Comfrey has probably been used as a healing aid for more ailments than any other herb. It is also considered to be an excellent animal feed. Some animals can consume vast quantities of comfrey; however, it has been found that **large doses of comfrey can cause liver damage** in humans. Externally, comfrey root can be grated and made into a poultice to treat bruising and swellings. It has been used in years gone by to treat broken bones.

RECIPE IDEAS

Although comfrey tea is sold commercially, in recent years, research has shown that comfrey taken internally can be detrimental to your health.

Small amounts of comfrey chopped in an omelet could work but overall, comfrey is better used as an external healing herb.

Comfrey ointment can be a helpful pain reliever when applied to aching joints, bruises, and sore muscles. To make your own ointment, chop washed and dried comfrey leaves. Add to melted wax or petroleum jelly and boil for about an hour. Pour liquid into sterilized jars through muslin to sieve. Be very careful when pouring. Wear protective gloves as hot wax is **very** hot.

Alternately, comfrey leaves make a great tonic for the soil in your garden and will help crops draw nutrients from the soil.

Ointment with comfrey.

DAISY (*Bellis perennis*)
(perennial)

There are thousands of different species of daisy. Perhaps the most commonly known is the lawn daisy (*Bellis perennis*), which is often considered to be a weed, but will decorate your lawn beautifully. Daisies are considered to represent innocence and are often associated with children. And as children are always drawn to them, this makes perfect sense! For centuries they have been collected as small posies to give to friends or made into daisy chains to hang around the neck or decorate the hair. The common lawn daisy is steeped in myths and legends and used to be known, in English, as "day's eye" because the flower opens and closes with the sun. The daisy has been used as a healing herb for many years and is known as one of the wound herbs. The plant aids in the healing process when applied to a fresh wound.

It's a hardy plant and will turn up uninvited on most lawns at some point. Daisies will start flowering early in the spring and carry on right through until the autumn and, in some areas, will even produce a flower or two in the winter months.

The low, flat leaves of the daisy plant will prevent other plants, weeds, and grass, from growing and will stay green all year in a moderate climate.

GROWING ADVICE

Daisies tend to come up in the garden whether you want them or not. Although considered to be a weed by many gardeners, the daisy is a useful herb to grow and is also a great source of entertainment for children of all ages. Lawn daisies are a hardy plant and can be mown down many times before they are defeated, if at all. The leaves grow low to the ground and prevent other weeds from growing.

If you do need to plant daisies, they can be started from seed. There are many different varieties of daisy, but the lawn daisy is one of the types considered to be an herb. Look for the seed for "lawn daisies" or "*Bellis perennis*." It's also a good idea to obtain fresh seed, as they will have a higher germination rate. The seed is usually collectable or available in summer and should be planted immediately if possible.

A field of beautiful daisies in bright sun.

Choose a sunny spot in the garden if you're preparing a special place for your daisies, although they will tolerate part shade. Daisies are very hardy plants, but they don't thrive if the soil is too dry or too wet. Make sure the ground is well-drained, never waterlogged, and kept watered during the summer if it dries out too much.

They are tolerant of all types of soil; rich, poor, acid, or alkaline, which is probably why they have a reputation among gardeners of being a weed. Dig over the ground and remove any perennial weeds and nonorganic debris. Rake over to a fine consistency and sow your seeds in lines. Check on your seed packet for regional growing recommendations. When the plants are large enough to handle, thin them to allow growing space of about 4–6" (10–15 cm) for each plant. Do this when the soil is damp to avoid damaging the roots. Water first if necessary.

If a very cold winter is expected, sow seed in pots during the autumn or winter months and keep warm and watered. When the ground is workable in the spring, plant out individual plants. Daisies are perennial and will come back every year, so choose your spot well in the garden before planting.

Other types of daisies can be grown along with the common lawn daisy, although they may not have the same properties and shouldn't be taken internally or used in medicinal preparations unless it's confirmed the plants are edible on the seed packet.

Many daisies propagate themselves by sending out new growth on runners, like strawberry plants. These can be separated off the main plant and

Container Growing

Although generally known as a lawn plant, daisies can also be grown successfully in containers. Plants spread, so pots should be quite large in diameter and well-drained. Daisies are used to rain and should be watered as much as possible during dry weather, although be careful not to waterlog the pots.

A delicious, fresh sandwich with arugula, cucumber, and olive oil, garnished and decorated with daisies.

repositioned. Separate the new plants after they have flowered. Daisy plants are often available in garden centers and suppliers. Check the variety before you buy.

HARVESTING AND STORING

Flowers and leaves can be dried, but daisies tend to be around for most of the year, so they can be used fresh as much as possible. Fresh leaves and flowers can be hung in a dark, airy, and dust-free place until completely dry and stored in sealed jars. Store out of direct light.

MEDICINAL USES FOR DAISIES

Daisies have been used as a medicinal herb for centuries. Preparations from the flowers are used to relieve mouth ulcers, coughs, and colds, and also to soothe patients that are in shock. A daisy tea will relieve the nervous system from stress and a handful of daisy flowers in a bath will melt away the tensions of the day.

RECIPE IDEAS

Add flower buds to salads and full flowers to decorate any dish.

Daisy leaves can be bitter, but young leaves are a good addition to salads or cooked as a vegetable. Steam lightly as you would spinach. Or make a lovely, fragrant bath tonic.

Wildflower Bath Tonic

Collect some or all of these garden wildflowers in any combination for a super tonic to relax in the bath. Note: Don't do this if you have plant allergies.

Ingredients
- Lawn daisies (flowers)
- Dandelions (flowers and leaves)
- Nettles (young leaves)
- Blackberry/bramble (leaves)

Directions
1. Crush your flowers and leaves together and place in a 7–8" square of muslin fabric. Bring up the edges to form a bag and tie securely.
2. Add a loop of string to hang over the hot water tap/faucet. Let the hot water run through the herb bag. Lie back and enjoy.

DANDELION (*Taraxacum officinale*)
(perennial)

Although nearly always considered to be a weed, dandelion is probably one of the most useful herbs grown today, privately as well as commercially. Every part of the dandelion plant can be used for either culinary or medicinal purposes. The root of the dandelion plant is used as a caffeine-free coffee substitute, the leaves are used in salads (and can be cooked like spinach), the flowers can be made into a delicious jam, and the stem holds a milky sap, which is considered to be a remedy for warts.

There have been many names, as well as myths, associated with dandelions over the years. One of the more well-known myths is that children wet the bed after picking the flowers. There is a grain of truth in this, as dandelions are a strong diuretic, although simply picking them doesn't have any effect at all! The common name, dandelion, is a corruption of the French *dents de lion*, meaning "lion's teeth."

Once established in a garden, dandelions can be hard to get rid of, so they must be positioned well, or they will come up randomly around the garden. Allowing flower heads to seed will spread the dandelions, which is why gardeners everywhere tend to discourage children from blowing the seed head away.

GROWING ADVICE

Propagating dandelions is not normally considered to be necessary, as they're a prolific "weed" and will turn up in most gardens at one time or another. However, gardeners have been trying to get rid of the plant for so many years, you may find the dandelion avoids your particular patch of ground.

Collecting dandelions from the wild is fine, but not advisable near roads or farmers' fields, unless it's an organic farm, because of the chemicals present in the air and soil. Always pick wild dandelions from environment-friendly areas, and always check before taking plants from the wild. Many areas are conserving the wild plant life and won't take kindly to someone arriving with a spade and digging up their plants, even if they are "just" dandelions.

Dandelions are a very hardy plant. If carefully dug up from one place, they can be replanted where you want them. Digging up a dandelion plant or two from wasteland or a nursery could be all you need to get dandelions established.

It's not always easy to come by the seed for dandelions, although wildflower seed suppliers should be able to help. Nipping the seed head off a plant and scattering it on your patch is worth a try. The seed head is the "clock"—the white fluffy ball that replaces the flower.

Because dandelions are such a widespread weed, they come up where they're happiest and aren't always easy to contain or germinate in the area you have allocated. However, to give them a good start, dig over the ground and remove any perennial weeds and nonorganic debris, then rake over the soil to a fine consistency. Gently scatter the seed and rake over very gently. Water. Pull out weeds until the dandelion plants are established. After that, they will look after themselves, although a little water in hot, dry periods helps to keep them growing well.

HARVESTING AND STORING

Dandelion leaves can be dried and stored to add to soups and stews, as well as herbal teas during the winter.

Dandelion flowers make a delicious jam, which can be kept almost indefinitely.

The roots should be collected from well-established plants. Dig around the plant carefully with a fork and ease the root out of the ground. Dandelion roots tend to be long and deep, so they will need to be carefully dug out to avoid being damaged. Choose a wet day or water the surrounding area first.

MEDICINAL USES FOR DANDELION

The milky sap inside the stem of the dandelion plant has been successfully used for many years as a treatment for warts and verrucae.

The leaves are a good source of vitamins and therefore, a good tonic in the winter months. Make a tea from the dried leaves.

The leaves contain vitamins A, C, and K, along with calcium, iron, manganese, and potassium.

Container Growing

Dandelions are rarely grown in pots, although they may come up on their own. It may be possible if the container or pot is well-drained and deep enough as dandelions have a long tap root. They use this root to find water in open ground and, if grown in pots, they should be watered regularly.

Dandelion spores can travel as far as five miles away!

Dandelion Jam

I learned this recipe from an old country woman in France and she was very particular about the number of dandelions used! Dandelion jam has many health benefits, from detoxifying the liver and aiding in digestion to being packed with vitamins, potassium, calcium, folate, and iron.

Ingredients

- 365 yellow dandelion flower heads
- 2 pounds sugar
- 2 pints water
- Juice of half a lemon or juice of a whole orange

Note: For a thicker jam, add 1x sachet of fruit pectin

Directions

1. First, you need to prepare the dandelion flowers. Wash thoroughly but carefully in cold running water. Then, pick out all the green bits. (These parts of the plant can be bitter. If you miss one here and there it's not a problem, though.) Prepare yourself for sticky yellow hands! Leave the dandelion flowers to drain for a few minutes.
2. Mix the water and sugar together in a large heavy-based pan and bring to a boil, stirring if necessary to avoid sticking.
3. Stir the dandelion flowers into the mix. Bring back to a boil, then simmer for 20 minutes.
4. Stir in the lemon or orange juice and simmer for another 2 or 3 minutes.
5. Remove pan from heat and allow to stand for 24 hours.
6. Pour mixture through a sieve into a new pan to remove the flower heads. Leave in a few petals for decoration.
7. Simmer mixture on a low heat for 20 minutes.
8. Stir in the pectin, bring back to a boil, and boil for 5 minutes.
9. Remove from the heat and let it cool slightly before pouring into warm sterilized glass jars. Label and date.

Note: Hot jam is VERY hot. Never pour hot jam into cold jars.

RECIPE IDEAS

Dandelion flowers can be made into dandelion jam or wine or even dandelion and burdock beer. The young leaves can be used in salads or as a spinach alternative. Use only young leaves, as the older ones tend to be very bitter.

And for caffeine reduction, the roasted root makes a warming drink.

DILL (*Anethum graveolens*)
(annual)

Dill has been around for centuries and was known to the ancient Greeks and Romans as a culinary and medicinal herb. The Romans saw dill as a sign of luck and the Greeks saw it as a sign of wealth. It also has a long culinary history in India. The name is derived from the Norse word *dilla*, which means "to lull." Dill has been used extensively to soothe and calm. In the Middle Ages, it was considered to be an effective charm against witchcraft. The idea was that if you could encourage a witch to drink dill tea, she would be too calm and soothed to be bothered with casting evil spells. Dill has been a main ingredient in gripe water for many years, and has proved itself as an aid to soothing indigestion, colic, and general digestive problems.

The seed is produced extensively all over the world. Dill pickle is probably one of the best-known commercial foods using this herb. Dill belongs to the same family as fennel and looks very similar, although the plants are smaller and don't produce a large bulbous root.

GROWING ADVICE

Dill is said to be one of the easiest herbs to grow successfully, so if you're a beginner in the garden, this is a good herb to start with.

Dill doesn't need to be started off indoors and should be sown *in situ*. Dill plants grow quite tall and should be positioned at the back of an herb or flower bed, but they like a sunny position and to be sheltered from the wind as much as possible. Position a few stakes in the ground before planting as supports.

Prepare a seed bed outside in the spring and rake to a fine consistency. Remove large stones and weeds and then sow your seed. Check on the seed packet for manufacturer's growing recommendations for your area, but you would normally plant the seed in mid to late spring, after the coldest nights are over and in time to get the early sun. Make successive small sowings every few weeks from spring to summer so you have a constant fresh supply of leaves. In regions with

***Dill should not be planted near caraway or
angelica. And although dill complements fennel,
they can sometimes cross-pollinate.***

mild winters, seed can be sown right through
until autumn.

Sow your seeds quite thickly so the plants
support each other in the wind, or thin the plants
out to allow about 8" (20 cm) of growing room
and support them with stakes. If you're using this
method, push the stakes into the ground before
planting as to not disturb the roots later.

Caterpillars can be a problem for dill, so keep
an eye open and hand pick them off if necessary.
Chemicals should never be used on plants that are
to be eaten. Keep your plants free of weeds and
they should grow without too much interference.
Outside plants will need watering in extremely dry
weather, but otherwise can be left to find water on
their own.

Container Growing

As with most herbs, dill can be
grown in containers or pots. Plants
do grow tall, so they will probably
need supporting with canes.
Position canes before planting
to avoid damaging the roots. Dill
has long tap roots which find
water more efficiently than other
plants. In a container, however, it
will regularly need watering. Make
sure the container or pot is fairly
deep to allow the roots to take up
nutrients from the soil properly.

HARVESTING AND STORING

The best way to keep herbs thriving and producing
leaf is to use them. Cut a few sprigs of dill
regularly and the plant will push out more foliage.

Dill leaves are best eaten fresh, but can be
dried and stored in airtight jars out of direct light
for several months, although there will be some
loss of flavor. The leaves can also be stored in a
refrigerator for a few weeks.

Collect the seeds and store in a jar for pickles
and vinegar making. The flower heads and seeds
are often used in making vinegars and oils.

MEDICINAL USES FOR DILL

Dill has been used to aid digestive problems
for many years, the most known use is in gripe
water for babies and young children. Make a
tea out of an infusion of dill leaves or crushed
seeds and drink after a meal to help soothe
stomach problems.

Dried dill seeds.

RECIPE IDEAS

The seeds of the dill plant are from the dried fruits and are usually added to homemade pickles. Dill seeds have a citrusy flavor and could be compared with caraway seeds.

The feathery leaves have a slight licorice flavor, but dill has a number of hidden flavors, making it a great addition to a mixed salad. Mix chopped leaves into a lettuce, onion, and feta cheese salad for a delicious alternative to a basic green salad.

Add chopped leaves to mayonnaise or tartar sauce.

Sprinkle over fresh fish before cooking.

Asparagus and Egg Salad

A unique spin on your average salad, swap out the leafy greens for more vegetables.

Ingredients

- Hard-boiled eggs
- Asparagus
- Potatoes
- Green beans
- Peas
- Dill

Directions

1. Gently steam all vegetables until just cooked and hard boil eggs.
2. Stir chopped dill leaves into cooled vegetables.
3. Once cooled, cut boiled eggs in half or quarters.
4. Arrange vegetables on a plate with the eggs on top.
5. Mix in some thinly sliced radish or onion to taste.

DOG ROSE (*Rosa canina*)
(*perennial*)

The dog rose is one of the wild varieties of the rose family and grows prolifically along hedgerows throughout Europe and elsewhere. Roses have been cultivated for over two thousand years and are known as "the queen of flowers."

All of the varieties in the rose family have similar medicinal properties, although the dog rose is highly valued for its prolific growth in the wild as well as the fruit of the plant, known as a rose hip. The rose hip is a good source of vitamin C and is used in cordials and syrups. It's considered to be a healthy drink for babies and young children. Rose hip tea is available in many supermarkets.

The dog rose grows rapidly and should be allowed quite a large space in the home garden to thrive, although it can be trained to climb over fences and other structures. The plant flowers in early summer, and the fruits can be harvested as they become ripe.

GROWING ADVICE

Dog rose plants are normally started with cuttings, although they can be grown from seed. The seed, however, may take up to two years to germinate. Cuttings can also take about 12 months to grow roots, but the rate of successful cuttings is high.

From Seed

Because the seed can take up to two years to germinate, the success rate tends to be a bit hit or miss. There are many factors that can lead to the seed not surviving over a long period: lack of heat and/or water, or too much of both. If you're determined to have a go, you need to be able to keep the trays in a very warm place and then allow them to cool down periodically.

If you sow the seed before it reaches full maturity, they can sometimes germinate slightly quicker and may come up in the following spring after autumn sowings. Use well-drained seed trays filled with

new compost and keep the soil moist. When the seedlings are large enough to handle, prick out into individual pots and look after them until they're strong enough to plant out in the garden.

Dog rose thrives on a sunny border (i.e. next to a low fence or hedge), although it will grow well in part shade. It can also be trained to grow as a hedgerow.

From Cuttings

Generally, roses are propagated by cuttings. Prune your plant back in the autumn after the last flowers and fruits have matured and have been harvested. Trim the cuttings and select the strongest and healthiest stems to use. Don't use stems that are diseased or damaged.

Cut the pieces you have chosen back to a few inches in length and push them into well-drained and fairly deep pots of new compost. Keep the soil damp, but not too wet. Cuttings and shoots can be kept in a cold frame until they have developed roots. Shoots could be ready the following spring, but may not be ready until later in the year.

Keep plants until the following year before planting out if they haven't established roots by the first spring. Cuttings can also be planted directly outside in a seed bed and moved to their permanent position later on.

Layering

Propagation from layering is also an option with the dog rose. The plant has long, trailing branches and is perfect for this kind of propagation. Choose a low branch that's strong and healthy and peg it to

Container Growing

Although most roses do well in pots and containers, the dog rose variety tends to grow long and straggly and is generally grown in open ground. However, with a large container and a support system in place, it may be possible. Make sure the container is well-drained but watered regularly.

the soil, where it naturally touches the ground, with a U-shaped peg. Cover with a light layer of compost and water well without disturbing the compost. Water in dry periods and keep weeds away.

When the new plant has developed roots, it can be cut from the main plant through the layering branch and then replanted or left to grow where it is. Cut back the branch remaining on the mother plant.

HARVESTING AND STORING

Dog rose petals can be dried and used in potpourri mixtures, although stronger smelling roses are normally used for perfume. Leaves can be dried by hanging in bunches or laying on trays in the sun, then crumbled and stored in a glass jar and used to make tea.

The fruits—the rose hips—should be made into syrups and cordials as soon as possible after harvesting, although they will keep for a day or two before they start to dry out.

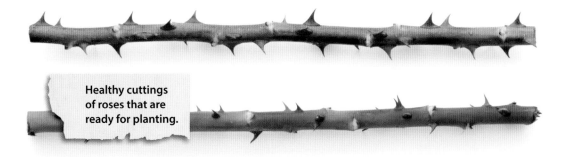

Healthy cuttings of roses that are ready for planting.

Drinking rose hip tea is a great way to boost immunity, reduce inflammation, protect against heart disease, and more.

MEDICINAL USES FOR DOG ROSE

The medicinal uses for all the plants in the rose family have been well-documented through the years. The fruits of dog rose—the rose hips—are probably one of the highest sources of vitamin C available, having many times, weight for weight, the vitamin C content of oranges and other citrus fruits. A cordial made from rose hips is a natural way to keep colds away.

Rose leaf tea is considered to be a calming drink and the leaves are a good tonic.

RECIPE IDEAS

Probably the most common use of rose leaf is in the form of tea. Simply steep leaves in boiled water for 5 minutes, strain, and serve.

Rose Water

Rose water is a wonderful addition to the food cupboard and can be mixed with drinks, smoothies, and many other recipes.

Ingredients
- 1 cup dried rose petals, or 2 cups fresh rose petals
- 5 cups water

Directions
1. If using fresh petals, wash and dry first and only use organically grown roses.
2. Put petals into a saucepan with water and bring to a boil.
3. Reduce heat and simmer for 20 minutes.
4. Leave to rest for an hour, then strain into sterilized jars.

Dried rose petals can be added to homemade soaps, face cleansers, body butters, and bath bombs. They are added to potpourri mixes, and fresh or dried petals are often candied and used as cake decorations. Uses of rose flowers, leaves, and fruits could fill a book and if you're growing these beautiful plants, research all the possibilities!

During the 1940s, rose hips were picked and used by families all over Europe, especially in the UK.

ECHINACEA (*Echinacea purpurea*)
(perennial)

Also known as purple coneflower, echinacea is known for its medicinal qualities and is widely used in many Ayurveda, herbal, and other natural healing preparations. It was used by Native Americans for hundreds, if not thousands, of years. Echinacea is native to mid-western America and was introduced to Europe in the nineteenth century. Echinacea is used in vitamin supplements and can be found in most health shops. The root has anti-bacterial qualities and has traditionally been the part of the herb used in healing and for boosting the immune system and treating colds. But in recent years, research strongly suggests that the flowers have healing qualities, as well as the roots.

In a high rainfall region, echinacea is better grown in a greenhouse or a place where it can be protected from too much rain. Find a hot and sunny position with fairly dry soil and this hardy plant will thrive. There are a number of varieties, but the purple coneflower (*Echinacea purpurea*) is probably the most widely grown.

GROWING ADVICE

Echinacea can be started from seed or root division. Ready-grown small plants are often available from garden suppliers. Echinacea likes a fertile soil, so if your growing soil is over-used or hasn't been used at all, dig in some well-rotted manure or organic fertilizer before planting.

Because echinacea originates from a hot dry climate, it won't tolerate too much moisture. If you live in a high rainfall area, the plants will need protecting. Choose a well-drained part of the garden or use a raised bed system with plenty of gravel or sand dug in for drainage. Dig over the ground and remove any perennial weeds and nonorganic debris. Rake to a fine consistency.

From Seed

Seeds can take up to six weeks to germinate and should be started indoors in the spring, but check on the growing recommendations on your seed packet for regional differences.

There is extensive research being done into the medicinal qualities of echinacea and to date, there seems to be a high success rate with treatments of various ailments.

High-quality echinacea seeds.

Start seed in well-drained trays or pots of new compost and keep slightly damp and warm until the seeds have germinated. When the seedlings are strong enough and the ground outside has warmed up, they can be transplanted into the garden in a prepared bed.

Water the pots well and ease out the weaker plants, leaving the strongest plant in each pot to grow on. Or, if they're to be planted out, transplant as soon as they've been taken from the pot. Use degradable pots to avoid damaging the roots.

Echinacea seed can be planted directly in a seed bed outside early in the spring. Again, check on the growing recommendations for your region. The seed should be sown around 2" (5 cm) deep and watered very gently. When the seedlings come up, protect from slugs, rabbits, and other wildlife. Echinacea shoots are very attractive to garden pests. Thin plants to allow around 18" (45.5 cm) of growing room per plant.

Root Division

Echinacea is easy to propagate by root division. In spring or late autumn, gently dig around the plant and lift the root, being careful not to damage it. The root can be pulled apart or cut into separate pieces and replanted. Each piece of root should be healthy and have fresh shoots. Replant quickly and water.

After the plant has been watered in, it should be regularly watered very lightly until signs of new growth appear. As soon as new growth appears and the plant is growing, water less often. A well-established echinacea plant shouldn't need watering again until late in the summer, and even then, only when the weather is particularly dry.

Never plant echinacea in wet ground. If the ground is getting too wet, protect the plant from further rainfall by covering with a large cloche to dry out the surrounding area of soil. The most important thing about echinacea is that although it's a hardy plant, it can't tolerate too much water.

Container Growing

Echinacea will grow successfully in well-drained pots, and this is often the best method when growing in a cooler climate or one with high rainfall. Pots can be moved around to capture the most sun during the day and brought indoors at night if the temperature drops. The plants need water, but be careful to never over-water.

Echinacea Tea

A cup of echinacea tea is a great immune system booster and combats cold or flu symptoms.

Ingredients
- Leaves and flowers of the echinacea plant
- Water

Directions
1. Bring a small saucepan of water to a boil and add leaves and flowers.
2. Simmer for 5 minutes.
3. Remove from heat and strain into a cup or jug over your preferred flavoring.
4. Stir and serve.

Note: Echinacea can be slightly bitter, so a sweetener or other flavoring can be added, such as honey, grated ginger, lemon juice, or even mint.

Echinacea will readily self-seed and produce seedlings around the mother plant every year. These seedlings can be replanted. Always allow about 18" (45.5 cm) of growing room. If the new seedlings come up more than 18" from the mother plant, leave them where they are unless you need the space for another crop.

Harvest the flowers as they bloom, and harvest the roots when the plant has finished flowering and is dormant. When digging up roots, try to limit the disturbance to the surrounding area, as the plant may have deposited seeds.

HARVESTING AND STORING
Seed can be collected from fully matured flower heads. Collect and lay the seed on paper for a couple of weeks until completely dry, then store in glass jars for planting next year. Label and keep out of direct light.

Roots should be washed then dried using a home dryer or in a very slow oven. When the roots are completely dry, they can be stored in a sealed container for up to a year, again out of direct light.

MEDICINAL USES FOR ECHINACEA
Echinacea has been proven to help stimulate the immune system and alleviate cold and flu symptoms.

The dried root is traditionally used for medicinal preparations, although research is showing the flowers contain similar properties.

Echinacea is also known to soothe skin conditions and is added to many herbal preparations. It is widely available as a supplement in health shops.

RECIPE IDEAS
Echinacea roots, leaves, and flowers are mainly used in healing preparations, but a cup of echinacea tea every day can boost your immune system and make you feel good.

FEVERFEW (*Tanacetum parthenium*)
(perennial)

Feverfew is a perennial and a fairly hardy herb that grows to about 2' (61 cm) tall. It produces many daisy-like flowers covering the plant throughout the summer months. It's sometimes confused with chamomile, but in fact, the flowers and leaves are very different.

As a member of the daisy family, and since the 1970s, much research has been done on feverfew and this family of plants. All members of the daisy family are known to have many medicinal properties. Feverfew is a well-known cure for headaches and migraines and has been used medicinally for over two thousand years, if not longer. The volatile oils in feverfew are stronger and more pungent than many other herbs and should be used in medicinal preparations with care.

GROWING ADVICE
Feverfew is easily started from seed and should preferably be sown in spring, although some autumn sowings will be successful if the oncoming winter isn't too severe, or the plants can be protected from the cold. Check the seed packet for growing recommendations for your region. Small, ready-grown plants are usually available in garden centers or from herb suppliers. Plants can also be started by root division and cuttings.

From Seed
Seed can be sown directly in the garden or in small pots to plant out later. Feverfew likes a sunny, well-drained spot in the garden and the ground should be dug over in the spring as soon as it can be worked. Remove any perennial weeds and nonorganic debris and dig in some well-rotted manure or organic fertilizer before sowing the seed. Rake the soil over to a fine consistency before sowing seed.

The seed can also be started in a seed bed. When the seedlings are large enough to handle, thin to about 2–3" (5–7.5 cm) between plants and then plant out later to their permanent positions.

Shown here is a young feverfew plant.

The plants grow to about 2' (61 cm) in height and possibly in width also, so place them where they won't shade lower-growing plants. Feverfew is a fairly hardy plant and will establish itself quickly in the herb garden. When the seed germinates and the seedlings are small, watch out for slugs. Use any organic method you can to avoid your new plants from being eaten.

If you buy ready-grown plants from a nursery, plant immediately unless the plants have been started in greenhouse conditions. If they have been cultivated inside, leave them in their pots for a few days. Put them outside during the day and bring them in at night before planting out to their final position in the garden.

Root Division

In late spring or early summer, carefully dig up the plant and with a sharp spade, cut the root into three or four pieces. Each piece of root should be a good size and healthy with no visible damage. Replant immediately and water in well.

Cuttings

Take cuttings in the autumn. Choose young shoots and cut below a "heel" in the stem. The heel will give the cutting a better chance of producing roots. By the next spring, the cuttings may be ready to transplant when the plant is obviously growing. If you gently tug the stem and it feels attached to the soil, there is likely to be a good root system already establishing itself.

If the cutting slides out of the soil easily, the roots (if any) probably won't be strong enough to plant out to their permanent positions in the garden yet. Wait a few months or until the following spring, keeping the cuttings protected in the winter and watered in the summer, until they have developed roots. Transplant all new plants to a sunny, well-drained position. Feverfew will die back during the winter months, but should come back in early spring. In extremely cold winters, a mulch of straw will help protect the roots.

Leaving a few flowers to dry on the plants may result in new seedlings the following year,

Container Growing

Feverfew is a good plant for container growing and will brighten up a patio with its cluster of flowers. Plant ready-grown plants in well-drained pots or containers and position in a sunny spot outside, or thinly sow seeds and pull out any weaker seedlings as they grow. Do this when the soil is damp. Water regularly but don't over-water. Watch out for slugs when plants are small.

depending on the winter conditions. Leave these to grow on, or gently lift when they're large enough to handle and transplant.

HARVESTING AND STORING

As with most herbs, fresh feverfew is stronger in smell and taste. The medicinal qualities are also more effective in fresh leaves. However, leaves can be dried in late summer to keep for the winter months. Dry on racks in the sun or in a home dryer, or hang in small bunches in a dry and dark place until crisp. Crumble into glass jars and label. Store out of direct light.

MEDICINAL USES FOR FEVERFEW

Both the leaves and the whole herb are used in medicinal preparations of feverfew. A topical tincture made from the leaves soothes insect bites and stings, and can be also eaten or drunk as a tisane to treat headaches and migraines, as well as being a useful tonic. It has also been used to calm nerves.

RECIPE IDEAS

The young leaves can be eaten raw or made into a tea with the flowers. Different types of daisy plants, including feverfew, have been used as stewing herbs over the centuries, as well as medications and flavorings.

Feverfew tends to be bitter, so it isn't often used in cooking, although small amounts are sometimes added to pastries and pies. The best way to enjoy feverfew for its medicinal properties (i.e. to relieve headaches and stress) is to make tea. Other herbs can be added for flavor.

Feverfew Tea

There are several other herbs you can add to feverfew herbal tea to make it less bitter.

Ingredients
- 1 tablespoon dried feverfew leaves
- Boiling water
- Optional: honey, lemon balm leaves, dried lavender, or other preferred herbs and sweeteners

Directions
1. Put dried feverfew leaves, or a small handful of fresh feverfew leaves and flowers, into a heat-proof jug.
2. Add any extra flavorings, such as lemon balm leaves, dried lavender flowers, and/or a spoonful of honey.
3. Pour boiling water on to the herb and leave to steep for 5 minutes.
4. Strain and serve.

LAVENDER (ENGLISH) (*Lavandula angustifolia*)
(perennial)

Lavender is probably one of the most well-known herbs and is grown all over the world. It has been used for centuries as a medicinal herb and at one time in history, it was used to flavor food because it was believed to help calm the stomach. Lavender has antiseptic qualities and has been used in medicines and ointments since Roman times. The ancient Egyptians used it in embalming fluids and placed lavender in the tombs of royalty. And the ancient Greeks used it to treat insect bites, stomach disorders, and kidney problems.

Lavender water was believed to cure fainting, nausea, and dizziness for many generations. It's also a favorite ingredient in detergents, air fresheners, and potpourri mixtures used in the home and workplace. Lavender clears the head and freshens the environment. Lavender flowers produce oil, which is used in many preparations, perfumes, and similar products. They're also a useful nectar-producing plant, which in turn yield high-quality honey.

GROWING ADVICE

Lavender grows as a small shrub, ranging from 6" (15 cm) to about 2' (61 cm) tall and prefers a sunny and dry position. Choose your spot well and lavender will continue to be a part of the herb garden for many years. Make sure the ground is well-drained. Lavender grows well in raised beds and resting on stone walls.

Lavender is happy to grow in most soils, but the optimum conditions would be dry, sandy soil that's not too acidic. Add a little lime before planting if you have acidic soil. Dig the ground well in the autumn before planting and remove any weeds and nonorganic debris.

Cuttings

The best method of starting lavender plants is from cuttings. Take cuttings of young branches from a well-established plant in late summer to early autumn. Make sure the branches have a "heel" and plant in a warm environment until the following

spring when they can be transplanted out in the garden. Dip the cut end in hormone gel or powder before planting, if available. Transplant in lines allowing space to grow, or simply plant one or two in a decorative area of the garden. A well-drained sunny spot anywhere in the garden will do.

Seeds
Lavender can also be planted from seed, but germination can be a bit erratic. Start the seed in well-drained pots of fresh compost and keep in a warm greenhouse or other bright and warm place. Keep the soil clear of weeds and water sparsely, but also keep slightly moist until germination. When the seedlings are strong enough to handle, transplant to the garden. Water sparsely, never allowing the plant to become too wet or the roots too waterlogged. When the plants start producing flowers in the first year of growth, cut them down to encourage growth in the main plant. The more foliage and new branches in the first year, the stronger the plant will become.

English lavender is the hardiest variety available and will tolerate very cold winters. If the ground isn't too wet just before winter, mulch to protect the roots from extreme cold. Remove mulch early in the spring. From the second year, let the flowers

Lavender seeds are just as beautiful as the plant itself with their purple tones.

grow. Lavender is a hardy plant and appreciates being used, so don't restrict yourself from cutting the stalks when required.

Lavender plants are aromatic and grace any garden left to their own devices. However, it's a good idea to pick it regularly to encourage growth and benefit from this wonderful herb. Trim to shape in the autumn if the shrubs are getting straggly and protect from severe cold. The English lavender variety will tolerate very low temperatures, but as mentioned before, a mulch can help it rest well during the winter months.

Container Growing

Lavender can be successfully grown in containers. Make sure they're well-drained and filled with fresh, organic compost. Don't use acidic soil in containers. Keep containers in a sunny spot outside on a patio or balcony and water sparingly. However, lavender is best grown outside in open ground, so keep an eye on the moisture level if growing in a container or pot and note how healthy your plants are before watering.

HARVESTING AND STORING
Lavender rarely needs storing, but the flowers are only available until late summer or autumn, depending on the variety. Pick flowers and dry them in the sun or a home dryer. Don't dry too quickly. The flowers can be stored in a glass jar. Use in recipes, potpourri mixtures, and drawer fresheners. Lavender products also make marvelous gifts.

MEDICINAL USES FOR LAVENDER
The medicinal uses for lavender would require another book to list them all. A sachet filled with dried lavender flowers and placed under the pillow will ensure a good night's sleep. Lavender

In the right environment, lavender plants can live for up to thirty years.

tea is helpful in alleviating stress headaches and migraines, as well as indigestion and colic. A few dried sprigs of lavender keep clothes, drawers, and wardrobes smelling fresh. If you're feeling industrious, sew a tiny cushion with dried lavender flowers inside. This can be popped in a drawer to freshen clothes or under a pillow to ensure a good night's sleep.

RECIPE IDEAS

Aside from all the homemade cosmetics that could benefit from a few lavender flowers thrown into the mix, lavender is also a useful culinary herb.

If you like the taste of lavender, you can add dried flowers to many recipes, especially cakes, biscuits, and even ice cream. Use in moderation.

Lavender Cookies

Inspired by French cuisine, these lavender cookies are a delicious treat!
(Makes 25–30 cookies)

Ingredients

- 1 cup self-rising flour, or plain flour with a teaspoon of baking powder
- ½ cup soft light brown sugar
- ½ cup butter
- 1 egg, beaten
- Grated rind of 1 unwaxed lemon
- Juice of 1 lemon
- ½–1 teaspoon dried lavender flowers, or to taste

Directions

1. Preheat oven 325°F (165°C). Grease baking sheets.
2. Cream the butter and sugar together until soft.
3. Beat in the egg, lemon rind, and lemon juice.
4. Crumble the lavender flowers into the flour evenly, then fold into the mixture to form a soft dough.
5. Using wet hands to avoid sticking, roll walnut-sized pieces of dough into balls. Place well apart on baking sheets and press down slightly.
6. Bake in a preheated oven for 20–25 minutes until the biscuits are spread and golden brown.
7. Leave on baking sheets for a minute or two, then transfer to a wire rack to cool completely.

LEMON BALM (*Melissa officinalis*)
(perennial)

Lemon balm is a shrub that normally grows around 2' (61 cm) tall. It is perennial, but the foliage dies back during the winter months. The bruised leaves release a fresh lemon smell, which makes it an excellent plant to grow next to pathways or seating areas.

Lemon balm originated in the Middle East, but is now widely grown throughout the world.

A popular preparation with lemon balm as the main ingredient was used throughout the seventeenth century and was known as Carmelite water. It was invented by Carmelite monks and nuns in the early part of the century in Paris and was used as *eau de cologne* and a cordial. Lemon balm leaves were infused with zest of lemon, coriander, nutmeg, and angelica root. Carmelite water was also taken to alleviate pain from neuralgia and nervous headaches.

GROWING ADVICE

Lemon balm is attractive to bees and in turn produces good quality honey. It's often found growing wild in light woodland and parkland areas where there's some shade. The plants should be placed in a sunny part of the garden that also gets a bit of shade, and somewhere permanent. Dig over the ground and mix in some rich, well-rotted manure or compost. Remove any weeds, large stones, and nonorganic debris. The leaves will die back during the winter, but the roots stay alive in the ground and, all being well, will shoot again in the spring.

In a very dry climate, lemon balm will do better in partial shade. In very cold winters, it may be wise to protect the plant by placing a garden fleece or cloche over it during the coldest months. Lemon balm is drought-tolerant once established and shouldn't need watering too often. It likes a light, well-drained soil. If the plant has ideal growing conditions, it will reseed itself and continue to get bigger as the years go by. It can be invasive, but parts of the root can be dug out to make room for other plants. When done carefully, this will not affect the main plant.

Cuttings

Lemon balm propagates well from cuttings. Take young cuttings in the autumn from an established plant and set out in the ground, leaving enough space for each plant to grow, approximately 12" (30.5 cm).

The cuttings can be started in a container, either as a permanent or temporary home. Not all cuttings will take, so it's a good idea to plant as many as you have space for. Dip the cut ends in hormone gel or powder before planting to help them along. The following spring, the cuttings should have produced roots. Discard the ones that haven't. Plant out the cuttings that have roots and are growing well to their permanent positions in July or August.

Root Division

Propagation can also be done by root division during spring or autumn. Dig up the plant very carefully to avoid damaging the roots. Separate into clumps and replant into containers or a seed bed until they become established and can be planted out into their permanent positions the following year.

Cuttings are a great way to propagate lemon balm.

Container Growing

Lemon balm grows well in containers and can be grown indoors, as well as outside. As it's a hardy shrub, it will thrive in most outdoor climates. Pots can be brought indoors or sheltered from very cold winters, but generally lemon balm will cope. The plants are also fairly drought-resistant and won't mind not being watered from time to time. Plants grow well on a windowsill, but constant hot sun may scorch the leaves, so a little shade protection may be necessary.

From Seed

Lemon balm can be started from seed, but germination can take some time and the seeds must be protected from birds, other wildlife, and weather conditions until they germinate. Sow the seed in well-drained seed trays of compost and keep in a cold frame. The seed can be sown in spring or autumn. As soon as the plants are large enough to handle, pot up and look after them until they're at least 6" (15 cm) tall when they can be planted out in the garden or permanent container. While getting established, lemon balm will need damp soil, but not wet. The plant won't cope with waterlogging and if grown in containers, it's very important the containers are well-drained.

HARVESTING AND STORING

Use leaves as often as required and harvest sprigs for storing just before or after the plant has flowered. Lemon balm leaves keep their scent

Lemon balm was once thought to cure all ailments and has long been used to relax and "soothe the nerves."

well and can be dried and stored successfully for many months in a glass jar, out of direct light. The plant produces lush foliage for a large part of the year and only needs to be stored for the winter months. The leaves are useful for lemon teas and potpourri mixes.

MEDICINAL USES FOR LEMON BALM

Lemon balm has several medicinal qualities. A lemon balm tea can soothe nerves and, when mixed with a little zest of lemon and a spoonful of honey, will help alleviate cold and flu symptoms. Fresh leaves are better than dried for making tea.

The leaves are soothing for insect bites and will deter mosquitoes if you rub the leaves onto your skin. A lemon tea at night is said to be relaxing and induces sleep.

RECIPE IDEAS

Lemon balm has a distinct lemon taste and can be added to all kinds of dishes, especially salads and fish recipes. It's also a great herb for flavoring homemade ice cream or fruit desserts.

Lemon balm tea is soothing inside and out! Simply pour boiling water over lemon balm sprigs in a jug. Let it steep for 5 minutes, then strain into a cup. Sweeten with honey to taste.

Lemon Balm Pesto

Try making this zesty lemon pesto, and feel free to add other leafy green herbs.

Ingredients
- 2 bunches fresh lemon balm; leaves and stems
- 2–3 tablespoons olive oil
- 1–2 cloves garlic, crushed
- Salt, to taste

Directions
1. Wash lemon balm and roughly chop.
2. Mix in a food processor with the olive oil.
3. Add the crushed garlic and blend until thoroughly mixed.
4. Season with salt to taste.

LOVAGE (*Levisticum officinale*)
(perennial)

Lovage is a hardy perennial plant and will last for many years, given the right growing conditions. It will also reach between 3– 7' (1–2 m) tall, so it needs to be placed at the back of a bed as to not overshadow lower-growing plants. Originally from Mediterranean areas, lovage has adapted to cooler climates.

Lovage has a strong taste (similar to celery) and is often used as a substitute for celery salt. The seeds are ground to make salt, and the leaves are used for flavoring stews and soups. The leaves can also be added to the salad bowl. Some cultures strip the outer skin off the plant and eat the stem raw as a vegetable, although generally the plant is used for its foliage and seed. Lovage has been used for many centuries in culinary and medicinal preparations, and it also has a high level of vitamin C.

GROWING ADVICE

Lovage is a hardy perennial and will survive fairly harsh winters. The foliage may die back, but will return in the spring, and while lovage likes a sunny spot, it will tolerate partial shade. The plants should be positioned at the back of a bed. It's not a suitable herb to grow indoors or in containers as it grows very tall. Plants can be grown against a fence or wall, as long as they have enough sun.

The ground should be well-drained and dug over well. Lovage likes a deep, rich soil, and well-rotted manure or compost should be dug in during the spring if you're planting the following autumn, or in autumn if you're planting in the following spring.

From Seed

Remove all weeds and large stones and rake to a fine consistency before sowing seed in the spring.

Ladybugs eat aphids and are a gardener's best friend. Leave old lovage stems in the ground so they can hibernate.

Ladybugs love lovage and will often hibernate in the stems.

Sow the seed, but check first with the supplier's growing recommendations, as there are a few different varieties.

When the seeds have germinated and the plants are big enough to handle, plant out into their permanent positions. Allow about 2' (61 cm) between plants. If you have too many young plants, try placing them in quiet corners around the garden or pot them up and give away as gifts. The seeds can also be started in well-drained seed trays full of rich seed or potting compost and planted out later. Keep your plants weed-free and watered until they become well-established.

Root Division

Lovage can be started off by root division. Dig up a healthy plant, carefully digging around the roots to avoid damage. This should be done in spring, just after the leaves start to show. The roots can be gently pulled apart and divided into two or more sections.

Replant the pieces that have a growing shoot in well-prepared ground, about 2' (61 cm) apart. Water and keep the ground moist while the plants get reestablished.

GENERAL GROWING TIPS

Create more foliage by picking off the flowers as they appear. Or, if you want the seed, allow flowers to fully ripen and then store or replant. The seeds are best sown when they're just ripe, which means an autumn sowing. In cooler climates, the young plants may need to be protected with a cloche or similar cover until the spring. Lovage grows well and will last a few years before the plant gets tired. At that point, root division can be a good way to restart your crop.

Container Growing

Generally, lovage isn't suitable for container growing, as it tends to grow very tall and prefers a deep soil. However, in a deep, well-drained container with nutrients added during the growing season, it may grow well. Repot every year if grown in containers and use fresh, organic compost. Roots can be divided every year when being repotted to propagate more plants. Position lovage containers behind low-growing plants to avoid overshadowing.

Potato and Lovage Soup

This creamy soup is perfect to warm up during those chilly winter months.

Ingredients

- 4 tablespoons lovage leaves, finely chopped
- 2 leeks, washed and finely chopped
- 1 pound potatoes, peeled and roughly chopped
- 3 tablespoons butter
- 4 cups chicken or vegetable stock
- Salt and black pepper, or preferred seasoning, to taste

Directions

1. Cook the leeks in 2 tablespoons of the butter in a large pan until soft, but not colored.
2. Stir in the lovage and potatoes and pour over the stock. Season and stir well.
3. Bring to a boil, then reduce heat and simmer until potatoes are cooked.
4. Remove pan from heat and allow to cool for a few minutes.
5. Push through a sieve or liquidize in a blender or food processor.
6. Reheat over a low heat, stir in the rest of the butter, and keep stirring until hot. Serve immediately.

Note: Use 2 small or 1 large onion instead of leeks for a stronger onion taste.

HARVESTING AND STORING

You can keep the seed to plant in the spring, although lovage seed does like to be sown soon after ripening. Seeds will need to be kept in an airtight container and out of direct light.

Lovage will die back in the winter, leaving a few collapsed stems which can be cut down. However, ladybugs like to hibernate in these stems, so leave them to die back naturally if you can.

The seeds of lovage can be stored for many months. The seeds can be ground and used as "celery" salt, and the leaves can also be dried and kept in a sealed jar—out of direct light—to add to stews and soups through the winter.

MEDICINAL USES FOR LOVAGE

Lovage has been used in many medicinal preparations for centuries and has been considered to be something of a wonder drug. It's known to stimulate the appetite and aid in digestion. At one time, it was also added to baths to deodorize and cleanse the skin.

RECIPE IDEAS

Lovage has a very distinct and intense celery-like taste. The chopped leaves can be stirred into salads and sauces and cooked into stews, casseroles, and soups.

MARIGOLD (*Calendula officinalis*)
(annual)

The *Calendula officinalis* plant is the original, old-fashioned "pot marigold" and has been traditionally grown in herb gardens all over Europe for centuries. Marigold was also used in early Indian and Greek cultures as a flavoring and a coloring for food. Native to southern Europe, the marigold has spread and now grows wild in some regions in the UK.

Marigolds are not only one of the best-known herbs, but they're also one of the most useful. The plant yields a yellow dye, as well as being an effective medicinal and culinary herb. It's also a helpful companion herb. Marigolds deter pests effectively and are often planted all over the garden amongst the vegetables and fruit crops, as well as in the herb garden.

Plants have bright yellow or orange blooms and will flower throughout the growing season. They're a must-have in the garden, both for their beauty and for all their benefits.

GROWING ADVICE

The true marigold (*Calendula officinalis*) is stronger tasting and has more medicinal qualities than the French and African hybrids (*tagetes*). Although these hybrids are worth growing, your true herb garden should include the *Calendula officinalis*. Marigolds are a magical plant to have in the garden. Spread them everywhere! They are sunny and bright, and they deter many pests, which keeps other crops bug-free. They also attract ladybugs, which is even better. No garden should be without them.

The one pest that will attack your marigold crop is the slug, so do anything you can to avoid having a slug problem. Hire in some toads or use a traditional method of deterring them. Broken eggshells laid around the plant helps, but is a bit laborious, or try a dish of beer—it attracts the slugs and then they fall in and drown. You may have a lot of drunk slugs to deal with in the morning, though!

Marigolds like a sunny spot, but will be able to tolerate partial shade. You can sow seed directly into the ground outside in late spring, but they will need thinning and spacing, so it's usually best to grow them in containers earlier in the year. Sow the seed thinly in seed trays of compost and water once. Make sure the trays are well-drained

Marigolds were believed to have magical qualities and were often used to decorate whole villages in times of celebration.

and keep in a sunny spot indoors or in a warm greenhouse until the plants have germinated and grown large enough to handle.

Marigolds germinate easily and shouldn't need to be watered again before they shoot, but keep an eye on the soil drying out if kept on a sunny windowsill. When the seeds have germinated, they will need a little water to keep them growing. The plants can then be transplanted into the garden when they are large enough to handle. Transplant your marigolds in sunny or semi-shaded areas of the garden. Scatter them around to protect other crops and to bring a splash of color all over the garden. Plant carefully and allow about 6" (15 cm) of growing room between plants if planting together.

Water your plants a couple of times a week, perhaps more if they're growing in a very dry environment. Mulching helps control weed problems. Remove flower heads as they die back to encourage more blooms, but a few flowers can

Container Growing

Marigolds grow very well in containers or pots. They will also be happy on a bright windowsill in the kitchen if you have the space. Plant seedlings in pots as soon as they're large enough to handle. The plants will need watering two or three times a week, depending on their position. Use well-drained pots of fresh compost to avoid weeds, and a little mulch will also help keep weeds down. Don't let pots dry out too much. Position large pots and containers around the patio, balcony, or garden to add a splash of color and use the fresh flower heads in the kitchen as they bloom to encourage more flowers to develop.

Marigold seedlings being cultivated.

be left to mature into seed development. The seeds can then be collected when ripe for resowing. Marigolds will start flowering in mid-summer and will carry on right through until the first frost. This is **not** a frost hardy herb.

HARVESTING AND STORING

Marigold flowers can be dried and stored in sealed jars for months, just make sure the flower is totally dry before storing. Dry by hanging in an airy, dust-free place out of direct light, or on a tray in a very cool oven for a few hours. If you have one, use a home dryer.

MEDICINAL USES FOR MARIGOLD

The medicinal uses for marigold are too numerous to mention them all, and it's been proven marigold has wonderful healing properties. These are a few remedies worth knowing about:

- If rubbed on the affected part, a marigold flower will soothe the pain and swelling of a bee or wasp sting.
- An infusion made from the leaves eases sore feet.
- Creams and lotions that are Calendula-based are highly effective in treating minor burns, wounds, inflamed areas of skin, and insect bites.
- Marigold flowers make a soothing tea.

RECIPE IDEAS

Marigold flowers have a citrusy, peppery taste and are worth adding to many dishes. They have been said to be the "poor man's" saffron and the bright yellow-orange petals certainly brighten up a plate of food. The leaves are edible, but have a strong, spicy taste.

Sprinkle a few fresh petals over a green salad and stir in gently. Use whole flowers to garnish almost any meal.

Sunny Fried Rice

Change up your rice routine with this unique and delicious side dish!

Ingredients

- 2 servings cooked rice
- 1 small onion
- 1 small red pepper
- 4–6 mushrooms
- 2–3 marigold flowers
- Oil for cooking

Directions

1. Wash pepper and mushrooms and chop into small pieces.
2. Peel and finely chop onion.
3. Heat oil in a large frying pan or wok and cook the pepper and onion for a minute or two.
4. Stir in the mushrooms and carry on cooking gently, stirring to prevent sticking for another minute or two.
5. Stir in the cooked rice and mix well. Carry on cooking until rice is hot. If the mix is too dry, add a little vegetable stock to the pan.
6. Add the marigold petals and stir gently for another minute or two.
7. Add seasoning if preferred.

Marigold petals can easily be added to any salad.

MINT (PEPPERMINT—*Mentha piperita*) (SPEARMINT—*Mentha spicata*)
(perennial)

Mint is probably one of the best-known herbs. The essential oil in mint is used in many medicinal and cosmetic preparations, as well as in the kitchen. Mint is a hardy perennial and a prolific grower. It's suitable to grow in pots and containers, as well as directly in the herb or vegetable garden in shady spots where nothing else seems to grow. However, it will rapidly take over a large area if not contained. Mint will often come back a couple of years after it's been "removed" from the area, so make sure it's planted where it won't disturb the rest of the garden.

Peppermint is the most popular and probably the most useful variety of mint. Peppermint can be used in sweet and savory dishes and is recognized as a healing herb. Spearmint and pennyroyal mint are also popular varieties to grow at home. There will usually be a choice of varieties available in your garden center.

Mint has been used as far back as Roman times and has been cultivated in Europe for many years, although there wasn't a lot recorded about the plant until the seventeenth century.

GROWING ADVICE

Mint will grow in virtually any spot and will take over the whole area if not checked. It's very suitable for container growing, but will also do well in a shady part of the garden where perhaps not much else will grow. Ideally, mint should be contained. Plant in a container that has been sunk into the ground, or alternatively in pots on a windowsill or outside on a patio.

Like most herbs, mint prefers a rich, well-drained soil but likes moisture, so a shady spot is ideal where the soil doesn't dry out too quickly. The area can't be waterlogged, though. Dig over

There are about 1,000 different types of mint, but only about five or six of these are worth cultivating.

To keep mint contained, it's best to plant in pots.

Mint is a hardy plant and doesn't need a lot of looking after, but a mulch occasionally will keep moisture in the roots, as they are shallow and can dry out quite quickly. This should only need to be done if the plant is growing in full sun or there hasn't been much rainfall.

Mint can occasionally suffer with a rust disease and should be pulled up and burnt if symptoms occur. Grow new plants away from the affected area. This disease can be caused by bad drainage, too much water, or a virus in the soil.

Pick leaves as you need them and remove the flowers to produce more foliage.

HARVESTING AND STORING

Hang sprigs upside down in a dust-free area in paper bags. The leaves can then be crumbled and stored in an airtight jar to be used for flavorings

the ground and mix in some well-rotted manure or compost during the season before planting.

It's very important to contain mint unless you want a field of it. Sink a bottomless container, such as an old bucket, into the ground or dig a deep hole and line with black plastic. This procedure won't completely contain the plant, but it will help. Alternatively, stick to container growing.

Mint will propagate easily from seed, as well as by separating the roots and replanting. Sow seed in early spring and keep moist and weed-free until the plants are large enough to handle. Then, pot them up or plant in the garden. To propagate by root division, simply break off the root and replant in potting compost until it has established a new root system and then plant out.

Garden centers and plant suppliers often have pots of mint ready to plant out. Look at the labels before buying—there are many different varieties available including *eau de cologne* mint, which isn't very suitable for mint sauce, but will produce a lovely scent in the home if grown indoors.

Container Growing

Mint is an ideal container herb and can be planted in small pots and kept on a windowsill. However, don't place in hot direct sun, as the soil will dry out too quickly and the leaves may become scorched through the glass. Keep pots of mint around the house, on a patio, or on a balcony. There are several different varieties that will flower and produce a lot of attractive foliage. Pots and containers must be well-drained and because mint likes a rich soil, plants will benefit from being repotted every year into fresh compost.

Pea and Mint Soup

Adding mint to soups is a great way to incorporate a refreshing quality and balance the flavors.

Ingredients

- 1 small potato
- 1 small onion or 2 shallots
- 1¾ cups peas
- 2 sprigs of fresh mint
- 2 tablespoons butter
- 1½ cups vegetable stock
- ½–¾ double cream or sour cream
- Seasoning of your preference

Directions

1. In a large saucepan, melt the butter over a low-medium heat.
2. Peel and chop potato into small pieces. Peel and chop onion or shallots.
3. Gently cook potato and onion over medium heat until soft, but not browned.
4. Add the peas, mint, and stock to the pan. Stir and bring to a boil.
5. Turn down the heat and simmer for about 5–10 minutes until the vegetables are cooked.
6. Remove from heat and allow to cool for 5 minutes. Remove the mint sprigs.
7. Blend in a food processor or blender until smooth and creamy.
8. Return to a clean pan and stir in cream and seasoning to taste. Reheat gently and serve.
9. Garnish with a few cooked peas and a sprig of mint.

Note: Mint can be finely chopped before adding to the pan and left in for an extra minty taste.

and mint tea. Label and store out of direct light. Mixing fresh leaves with vinegar is another way to store mint. Again, keep in sealed jars.

MEDICINAL USES FOR MINT

Mint is well-known for its medicinal qualities and is regularly drunk as a tea or eaten in the form of a candy after meals to aid digestion.

Many people swear by a cup of mint tea every day to keep colds and the flu away. It's also a great remedy for headaches and stress.

RECIPE IDEAS

A daily cup of mint tea is refreshing and good for digestion. As with all herb teas, put a fresh sprig or two of mint in a jug and pour over boiling water. Let it steep for 5 minutes, then strain and serve, adding a little honey and/or lemon juice if preferred.

OREGANO (*Origanum vulgare*)
(perennial)

Oregano is also known as wild marjoram. Both herbs belong to the *Origanum* family, but they are different plants. Oregano originated in the mountains of Greece and was thought to produce a more flavorsome meat from the goats that grazed on it. It spread across the Mediterranean area and now grows well in many regions of the world. The herb grows wild in many parts, especially in Southern Italy, and is a viable commercial product in Europe and Mexico.

Oregano grows as a low bush and in mild climates, it will stay green throughout the year. As with any leafy herb, the strength of flavor and aroma greatly depend on the temperature and water supply. Oregano is packed with minerals and vitamins and plays a strong role in healing minor ailments.

GROWING ADVICE

Oregano plants last three or four years before they need replacing. The seeds tend to germinate well. One way of sowing seed is by sprinkling onto pots of warm compost and spraying with water daily, probably two or three times a day. You can start the seeds off like this quite early in the year, as long as they're kept warm. Keep the pots in a greenhouse or on a sunny windowsill, but make sure they don't get too much sun before germinating. It's also important to keep the soil moist.

When the plants are large enough to handle, thin out to allow enough space for them to grow. If you're keeping them in pots, pull out the weaker one and leave only one plant per pot. (Sow two or three seeds per pot if you intend to do this.)

Oregano is well-suited to container growing and will grace a patio, brighten up a kitchen windowsill, or look stunning in a hanging basket. It will also enhance an herb or vegetable garden.

Oregano has startling bright leaves and provides a pretty ground cover, as well as deterring pests from a veggie patch. Grow a few plants around sweet peppers to provide the humid atmosphere peppers thrive on.

Oregano was considered to be of high medicinal value in Roman times, and for centuries has been used in medicinal preparations.

Once it's tall enough, oregano loves to be cut and used and it will continue to grow back!

In late spring, or after all danger of a frost has passed, oregano seed can be sown directly outside. Sow in a well-drained seed bed and keep watered and weed-free. Thin the young plants out when they're large enough to handle to give them enough space to grow. A well-established oregano plant may spread to a few feet wide, but they can be trimmed back if too unruly. It's a good idea to check on the recommended growing instructions on your seed packet if you have one, as varieties differ. Times of planting are affected by your region's climate and some hybrid varieties will need more space than others.

As soon as the seeds have germinated, reduce watering. Oregano should never be watered in damp conditions. The foliage dies back in the winter, but will return the following spring. In very cold winters, it's advisable to protect your plants with mulch. If you live somewhere that has severe winters, you may consider growing herbs in containers that can be brought inside during the cold months.

The plant can be trimmed back and shaped, although this can be carried out as you use it. Use oregano often and it will produce more leaf. Pick the flowers off when they appear to produce more foliage. If you want the plant to flower, harvest plenty of leaves before the flowers start to appear. Pick just a few leaves until the whole plant is about 8" (20 cm) high, then cut as much as you want and it will keep growing back.

Oregano is a wonderful herb for deterring aphids, including green and black fly. Position your oregano plants in sunny spots around the garden to help keep aphids away. Oregano's beautiful foliage also provides spectacular focal points.

HARVESTING AND STORING

Oregano can be dried by hanging upside down in brown paper bags and then crumbled and stored in sealed glass jars. Keep out of direct light. The

Container Growing

Oregano is an ideal container plant and will happily grow in a pot on a windowsill or any bright spot indoors. The most important thing about growing oregano in pots or containers is making sure they're well-drained. Put a layer of gravel at the bottom of the pot to ensure good drainage.

Oregano Open Sandwich

Oregano is often used in Greek cuisine, and this sandwich is sure to reach those Mediterranean tastebuds!

Ingredients

- Fresh oregano leaves
- 1 small onion
- Juice of 1 lemon
- Olive oil
- Salt, to taste
- 1 avocado, sliced
- A few black olives
- Feta cheese, sliced
- Sliced bread, preferably sourdough

Directions

1. Finely chop onion and mix with oregano leaves in a medium to large bowl.
2. Pour the lemon juice into a separate bowl and slowly whisk in the olive oil to make the dressing.
3. Taste and add seasoning as preferred.
4. Stir dressing into oregano and onion.
5. Lightly butter the bread (optional) and lay slices of avocado and feta cheese on top. Add olives and lightly drizzle with dressing. Serve.

herb is also available fresh for much of the year and, as with most herbs, the taste does deteriorate with drying.

MEDICINAL USES FOR OREGANO

Oregano is used in preparations to soothe sore throats and coughs in children. It has been used in digestive cures, as well as many other general disorders, including influenza. Oregano is also a highly effective antiseptic and has sedative qualities. **Large doses should not be taken.**

RECIPE IDEAS

Oregano has a strong, spicy taste and has been compared to mint, but the two herbs are not interchangeable in recipes. To remove the leaves for cooking, hold one end of an oregano sprig and run your thumb gently but firmly along stem.

This is a great herb to enhance a roast chicken dinner. Mix fresh oregano leaves with lemon juice and crushed garlic. Gradually drizzle in some olive oil, whisking all the time. Rub the mixture into the chicken before cooking.

PARSLEY (*Petroselinum crispum*)
(*biennial*)

Parsley has traditionally been used for food garnishing and flavoring, for headdresses, and even for adorning tombs during ancient Greek times. Parsley originally grew wild in Mediterranean areas, but has been cultivated throughout Europe and America for many centuries.

It is probably the most underused herb in the garden, but is rich in vitamins and minerals, particularly iron.

There are a number of different varieties. The most commonly used are the curly leaf and Italian flat leaf types, which are added to many recipes, as well as being an attractive garnish. In recent years, the remarkable properties of parsley have been well-documented, and the herb is freely used in professional and home kitchens, although there is still a temptation to use it only as a garnish.

GROWING ADVICE

Parsley likes to grow in a sunny spot and thrives in a rich soil. It grows well in containers and can be dotted around the garden to grow with other herbs and vegetables. Varieties of parsley differ so much that it's hard to tell if they come from the same family sometimes. Try growing flat leaved and tight curly leaved varieties to compare.

Buy ready-grown young plants from a nursery or garden center to get your crop going quickly. These plants are often started in forced conditions and aren't hardened to cold nights. Keep plants on a sunny windowsill and keep well-watered. They may be transplanted a little later in the year, although a healthy parsley plant will keep green and fresh right into the winter months on a sunny windowsill. Always ensure pots are well-drained, but parsley needs to be kept moist, so water regularly.

Choose a well-drained sunny spot outside. Parsley will tolerate some shade, but the soil will need to be rich in nutrients for it to thrive. Dig over the ground and remove any perennial weeds, then dig in some well-rotted manure or rich compost, if available, before putting out your parsley plants.

Gram for gram, parsley has more vitamin C than citrus fruits.

From Seed

Parsley will grow readily from seed, but can take more than six weeks to germinate, so it needs to be started in clean compost where the seeds won't be drowned with weeds. Some growers soak the seed for 24 hours before planting to speed up the germination process.

Sow a few seeds in pots and keep warm and the soil moist. When the plants come up, thin to one plant per pot. The seedlings you remove can be planted elsewhere, but consider how many parsley plants you may need. The "thinnings" may be better off in the salad bowl.

Seeds can be planted directly outside, but not until the weather is warmer. Parsley needs a long growing period, so it's generally better to start them in early spring in a greenhouse or indoors. When all danger of a frost has passed, young plants can be transplanted into the garden and containers can be put outside.

Always wait for warm weather to plant parsley seeds outside.

Container Growing

Parsley grows well in containers, but must never be allowed to dry out. Use well-drained pots of fresh compost and sow seeds sparsely or plant out with one or two ready-grown plants, depending on the size of the pot. In colder climates, a pot of parsley can be kept indoors over winter and will often produce leaves until the following spring. Try growing a couple of varieties in each pot (size permitting) and position in a sunny spot. Remember to water regularly in dry weather.

Parsley is a heavy feeder, resulting in iron and mineral rich leaves. If your soil could be lacking in nutrients, parsley will benefit from a regular organic feed. Start using the leaves when the plants are at least 8" (20 cm) tall and use all through the year. During the second year of growth, parsley will produce flower and seed. The seeds can be collected when ripe.

Parsley has a long tap root and tends to look after itself well once it settles in, but it should never be allowed to dry out. Water regularly in dry weather.

HARVESTING AND STORING

Use leaves when required as soon as the plant is established. For seed collection, hang flower heads upside down in a paper bag when the seed has started to form. Leave in a dry, airy place until the seeds drop from the rest of the plant, then store

Parsley Pie

This is a traditional Cornish recipe, especially good for using up leftovers.

Ingredients
- Enough fresh chopped parsley to almost fill an oven-proof dish
- Pie crust
- A little stock
- Leftover cooked meat and/or vegetables, chopped
- Boiled eggs, chopped

Directions
1. Preheat oven to 350°F (177°C).
2. Lightly grease an oven-proof dish. If you prefer a pastry base, line dish with pie crust and bake blind until pastry is set, but not cooked through.
3. Mix together chopped fresh parsley and cooked lamb or any other meat or vegetarian substitute (chopped or minced).
4. Add a couple of chopped hard boiled eggs and any chopped veggies you may have lurking in the fridge.
5. Season and pour a little stock over the whole lot. Don't make it too wet or the pastry will be soggy. The stock could be meat, chicken, ham, or vegetable.
6. Cover with a pastry top and bake in the preheated oven for about half an hour.

Note: When reheating meat, always make sure it's piping hot right through before serving.

seed in a sealed jar. Remember to label the jar and store out of direct light.

To dry parsley leaf, hang the whole stems or lay on racks to dry, then crumble leaves and store in sealed jars. Label and again, store out of direct light. Whole stems of parsley can also be frozen.

MEDICINAL USES FOR PARSLEY
Because of its high iron content, parsley is thought to strengthen the blood. It also has high quantities of vitamin C and is therefore a healthy herb to use as a vegetable. Parsley also freshens the breath and is a must-have with garlic bread!

RECIPE IDEAS
Although parsley has been used as a garnish for many years, it's now being recognized as a valuable food. Try the recipe above for a Parsley Pie!

ROSEMARY (*Rosmarinus officinalis*)
(perennial)

At various times throughout history, rosemary has been burned to ward off evil spirits, its smoke has been inhaled to cure colds, and it's been mentioned in countless fairy stories. It's also been used in blessings and ceremonies, such as baptisms and weddings.

Rosemary has been cultivated in kitchen gardens for centuries and is an herb that's nearly always seen in gardens. One of the great advantages of rosemary is that it's a hardy perennial and will last for up to twenty years with just a little care and attention. Although originally from Mediterranean areas, rosemary has become hardier the farther north it travels. It can be used throughout the year and will stay green even in cold winters.

Rosemary is an evergreen plant with leaves resembling pine needles which can be chopped and used in recipes, although many cooks simply add a sprig of rosemary to the cooking dish.

GROWING ADVICE

Rosemary can be grown from seed, although it isn't always easy to germinate. The best way to get a rosemary plant started is by the "cuttings" method. Rosemary likes a sunny and sheltered spot. The plant should be positioned in a place where it won't be damaged by strong winds. It will last through most cold winters, but wind and rain along with low temperatures, could kill the plant.

From Seed

Sow all the seed you have and have a plan B! Start the seed in trays or pots of seed compost. They must be well-drained. Keep the surface of the compost moist, but never waterlogged. Seed can take up to three months to germinate. The pots or trays need to be kept warm until seedlings are ready to plant out.

Patience is key in growing rosemary from cuttings.

Sowing from seed is not the usual form of propagating rosemary, and recommended growing instructions on the seed packet may give some extra tips to getting a good germination rate. When the plants are large enough to handle, they can be transplanted into the garden or containers. Rosemary is happy to grow in containers, although the plants do grow fairly large, so a spacious pot is required.

Rosemary has been known to tolerate near-drought conditions, but it needs water during hot, dry periods to thrive. Watering will keep it growing and make it usable for longer in the year.

It's unlikely that you'll need more than a couple of good, established rosemary plants, but they're attractive and don't take up much time or space, so it's worth thinking about planting a few extra. If you're tight on space though, just get one or two plants thriving and it will be plenty. As with all herbs, rosemary likes to be used.

Cuttings (Plan B!)

Although you may only want one or two rosemary plants, when you plant cuttings, allow a few more, as some may not take. The most successful way to propagate rosemary is to take 3–4" (7.5–10 cm)

cuttings just above or below a leaf joint from a healthy plant. Then, push the cuttings into pots of potting compost. Dip cut end in hormone gel or powder if available.

Keep the pots warm and use a propagator if you have one, or simply cover the pots with plastic or glass until the roots have established. The cuttings will take about two months to grow roots and they should then be carefully transplanted into the garden or larger containers. Position in a sunny spot.

In a region with mild winters, a seed bed is a good area to get cuttings started because the soil is usually finer and more maintained than other parts of the garden. Wherever you plant the cuttings, make sure the ground is well-drained and protected from extreme cold. Rosemary tolerates fairly poor soil, but it doesn't particularly like acidic soil. Add a little lime to the ground before planting out if the soil in your garden is particularly acidic.

Container Growing

Rosemary grows well in containers and doesn't mind drying out occasionally, although to keep your plants fresh and green, water regularly, especially in hot, sunny periods. Always use well-drained pots or containers and fill with non-acidic soil. Shrubs can grow fairly large, so adequately sized pots will ensure the plants grow well. Rosemary flowers every year and stays green throughout the year, so it makes an attractive patio or balcony plant. Choose a sunny spot out of cold drafts.

Rosemary and Garlic Focaccia

This bread recipe is simply a must-try and will surely become a new favorite!

Ingredients

- 1 pound + ¼ cup strong white bread flour
- 1½ teaspoons dried (instant) yeast
- 1 teaspoon salt
- 1½ cups lukewarm water
- 3–4 tablespoons olive oil
- 2 large or 4 small garlic cloves, finely chopped
- 1 teaspoon flaked salt
- Black pepper
- Needles from 3–4 rosemary sprigs, finely chopped

Directions

1. In a large bowl, stir the flour, yeast, salt, and water together and mix to a soft dough.
2. Knead for about 15 minutes by hand or use a mixer with a dough attachment.
3. Clean and grease a separate bowl. Place the dough in the bowl and cover with cling film.
4. Leave in a warm place to rise for 30 minutes.
5. Preheat oven 450°F (230°C).
6. Slightly warm and line a baking tray and spread dough on the tray.
7. Drizzle about 2 tablespoons of olive oil over the dough. Top with rosemary, garlic, and flaked salt to taste.
8. Press fingers into the dough to make dimples and leave to rest again for 30 minutes.
9. Bake for about 15 minutes until golden brown, turning the tray halfway through cooking.
10. Remove from the oven, drizzle a little more olive oil all over, and leave to cool.

HARVESTING AND STORING

As rosemary is an evergreen, it's available fresh all year-round, but it can be dried. Hang sprigs up inside a paper bag to collect the needles as they fall. Note that drying rosemary will reduce the strength of the flavor and scent.

MEDICINAL USES FOR ROSEMARY

Rosemary leaves are used in an infusion to soothe digestive problems, stress, headaches, and a number of other ailments.

The oil is externally applied to insect bites and is also widely used in the cosmetic industry.

Rosemary leaves can be added to a bath to relax nerves and tension. Sew some into a small muslin bag and hang from the tap while the water is running.

RECIPE IDEAS

Add rosemary sprigs to chicken, potatoes, and other vegetables. Remove after cooking.

Dried rosemary should be used in moderation to avoid overpowering other tastes.

SAGE (*Salvia officinalis*)
(perennial)

Sage originates from southern Europe, and although it's a hardy perennial, it should be replaced approximately every five years.

To the Ancient peoples, sage was considered to be an herb of wisdom, good health, and psychic powers, among other things. It was used in medicinal preparations to treat infections, memory loss, fevers, and stomach problems. Sage has been used medicinally for thousands of years and has also been used to flavor food for a similar amount of time.

Sage originated in the Mediterranean, but is now widely grown. There are many varieties available, including variegated types grown for both decorative and culinary purposes. It's mostly grown for culinary use, but is still used medicinally by herbalists and alternative remedy enthusiasts with good results.

GROWING ADVICE

It's more satisfying to grow sage from seed, but you will have to wait over a year before you can use it. Alternatively, you can buy small ready-grown plants from a nursery or garden center or start your plants from cuttings or layering from an established plant.

From Seed

Sow your seed in early spring in seed trays or pots of new compost. Keep damp but not too wet, and make sure the containers are well-drained. Sage is native to Mediterranean regions, so it doesn't need a lot of watering.

Put plants out into their permanent positions a bit later in the year and keep them protected. Check on the growing recommendations on your seed packet because there are a number

of different varieties and some may suit your region better than others. Growing from seed usually allows for more of a choice, and there's no reason why you shouldn't grow different varieties. Variegated types will add a touch of color and design to an herb garden or vegetable patch.

Layering

Sage is often propagated by layering. Because it's a woody shrub, the stem will produce roots. Layer from mature, well-established plants in the spring or autumn. Peg healthy, lower stems down and cover with about half an inch of soil. Water and leave to develop roots. Once the plant is firmly established, the layered stem can be cut from the mother plant and the new plant transplanted as required.

Sage doesn't need a lot of watering or maintaining.

Container Growing

Although a hardy plant, sage doesn't like long, cold, wet winters, so if grown in containers, it can be brought indoors during these months. Sage thrives in a container, as long as it's well-drained and large enough. Plants can get very woody after a few years and should be replaced, if necessary, but a healthy sage plant in an ideal spot can last for many years. Sage is an attractive container plant for a patio or balcony, and the new variegated types create an attractive display. The soil shouldn't be allowed to dry out completely, but never over-water sage.

Cuttings

Take 3–4" (7.5–10 cm) cuttings from a well-established plant in spring or summer and push them into potting compost in a well-drained container. Dip the cut ends in hormone gel or powder before planting if possible to give the cuttings a head start. Keep warm and watered, but not too moist.

The containers or pots should be kept in a sheltered spot, away from wind or frost pockets. Once the cuttings have taken root and are starting to grow, they can be transplanted into larger containers or out into the herb garden.

Later in the year when the flowers have died back, the plants can get straggly. Prune back to the shape you want them. Early summer is usually the best time, as sage flowers in the spring, although flowering times can vary with different varieties and regions. There are new hybrids that have beautiful foliage but are reluctant to flower, so make sure you know which type you are buying.

Sage is a fairly hardy plant and will survive most winters, although they may not survive a very

Sage and Onion Stuffing

Sage and onion stuffing has been available dried in packet form for many years, but it's extra tasty when homemade from scratch!

Ingredients

- 4 medium onions
- 10 sage leaves
- ½–¾ cup breadcrumbs
- 4 tablespoons butter, softened
- 1 egg yolk
- Salt and pepper, to taste

Directions

1. Peel onions. (Make sure they're crisp and have no damaged or soft parts.) Put them in a pan and cover with water. Bring to a boil, then reduce heat and simmer for about 10 minutes or until the onions are cooked.
2. In the last couple of minutes of cooking time, add sage leaves to the pan. Drain well and allow to cool for a few minutes.
3. Finely chop onions and sage and place in a large bowl. Stir in breadcrumbs and softened butter. Mix well and bind with egg yolk. Add salt and pepper to taste.
4. Shape into balls to make individual portions and bake on a baking sheet in a preheated oven (375°F, 190°C) for 20 minutes or until slightly crisp.

long cold spell. The plants will suffer if the roots are too wet. Containers are a good idea if you have particularly cold and wet winters. Bring the containers in before the first frosts and keep them indoors until spring.

Sage thrives in well-drained soil in a partly sunny, partly shady position. A walled herb garden is ideal, or plant some near rocks or in a rockery. When kept trimmed, sage will grace a rock garden for years.

HARVESTING AND STORING

Some sage flower varieties can be picked in spring and candied. The leaves can be dried and stored in sealed jars. Hang stems or lay on racks in a dust-free environment until dry enough to crumble before storing. Label the jar and store out of direct light. The leaves can also be frozen and sealed in freezer bags. In milder climates, sage can be picked fresh for most of the year.

MEDICINAL USES FOR SAGE

Sage has been used in medicinal preparations for centuries and is commonly known today to reduce menopausal night sweats.

Sage has volatile oils which can be prepared into very effective medicinal aids, although the oils do contain toxins, so sage should never be taken in large doses.

RECIPE IDEAS

To make a sage tea, simply steep a few leaves in hot water, just after boiling, for about 5 minutes. Add a spoonful of honey if preferred.

SAVORY (SUMMER SAVORY—*Satureja hortensis*) (WINTER SAVORY—*Satureja montana*)
(Summer savory is an annual and winter savory is an evergreen perennial)

Both summer and winter savory have the same medicinal and culinary properties, although winter savory is coarser and stronger tasting. Both types have been prized for their flavoring over their medicinal qualities for many years, but its medicinal qualities are well-documented.

Savory has been used for thousands of years as both a medicinal and culinary herb and was cultivated throughout Europe from the ninth century. Savory was used as a love potion for many years and is mentioned throughout history in herbal and medicinal books. It is native to Southeast Europe and North Africa, but is now widely grown throughout Europe and other parts of the world. Savory is used extensively in French cuisine and is one of the mixture of herbs known as *fines herbes*.

Summer savory is an annual plant and grows to about 12–15" (30.5–38 cm) high and has pale lilac flowers in the summer. Winter savory is an evergreen perennial. It grows as a hardy shrub

and in milder climates, the leaf can be used right through the winter months.

Savory is likened to thyme and marjoram for its flavor and appearance.

GROWING ADVICE

Summer savory is raised from seed every year and winter savory can be started from seed, cuttings, or root division. Although winter savory is a perennial plant and will keep growing for a long time in the right conditions, after a couple of years, it will start to become woody and produce less foliage. Therefore, it's a good idea to replace winter savory every two or three years.

Summer Savory from Seed

Summer savory likes a sunny position and a fairly rich, light soil. If the soil is heavy, dig in some sand or light gravel before sowing. Dig over and prepare the ground as early as possible and incorporate some well-rotted manure or organic

Be careful not to cut the stems too far—this will result in taking the plant longer to recover.

fertilizer. Remove any perennial weeds and rake to a fine consistency. Sow seed in early spring in shallow drills about 9–12" (23–30.5 cm) apart.

Savory seeds are notoriously slow to germinate. When the seedlings are large enough to handle, around a couple of inches in height, they will need thinning. Choose a wet day or water the ground well first if it's dry. Gently pull out weaker seedlings leaving about 6" (15 cm) of space for each plant. The thinned-out plants can be transplanted to another bed. Water well after transplanting. Keep the soil damp and remove weeds by hand as they appear.

Seeds can also be scattered over a prepared bed, but will still need thinning to allow space for the plants to grow. Wait until the plants are large enough to handle before thinning.

Winter Savory from Seed

Seed should be treated as summer savory, but check on the seed packet for growing recommendations for your region before sowing. Winter savory is a low-growing shrub and can be positioned at the front of most herb, flower, or vegetable beds. It can also be a good border plant.

Winter Savory from Cuttings

Choose fresh shoots in the summer months and cut just below a "heel" in the stem. Plant in a seed bed or well-drained pots of fresh compost. Dip cut ends in hormone gel or powder if available to help speed up root growth. Keep soil damp, but not too wet, and remove any weeds as they appear. When the cuttings have developed roots, they can be replanted in the garden.

Cuttings can be encouraged to produce roots faster by keeping them protected in a greenhouse, but they'll usually be fine if planted directly outside. Plant more cuttings than you need to allow for those that don't take.

Winter Savory from Root Division

Dig up a well-established plant in the spring and pull the root apart into several pieces. Immediately replant pieces in prepared soil.

Use savory as soon as the plants are growing well and are about 3" (7.5 cm) tall. Take just a few leaves from each plant until they're

Container Growing

Savory can be successfully grown in well-drained pots and containers, but they should be at least 12" (30.5 cm) in diameter, as plants tend to grow bushy. Place pots in a sunny position. Don't let the pots dry out and water regularly in dry weather.

well-established. As mentioned above, winter savory can get woody and straggly after two or three years and may need replacing.

HARVESTING AND STORING

Summer or winter savory can be used fresh for most of the year. Winter savory should produce foliage through part of the winter, depending on the severity of the temperatures and the amount of rainfall. Summer savory should be pulled up when the plant is in flower and the whole plant hung upside down in bags in a dark and airy place until dry. Store dried leaves in jars out of direct light. Remember to label.

MEDICINAL USES FOR SAVORY

Because savory is a warming herb, it has often been used to aid digestion and reduce flatulence. It's also an effective expectorant for relieving coughs and bronchial disorders.

Fresh leaves have also been known to soothe wasp and bee stings.

RECIPE IDEAS

Savory has a warm, peppery taste and can be used as a condiment if pepper is unavailable. Summer savory has a lighter, spicier taste and winter savory is more earthy. Both can be rubbed into meat before cooking.

Savory Meatballs

Whether you have a go-to meatball recipe or not, you'll want to add this one into the mix!

Ingredients

- 1 pound ground beef
- 1–2 onions
- 1–2 garlic cloves
- 4 tablespoons fresh breadcrumbs
- 1–2 tablespoons chopped fresh savory
- 1 egg yolk
- Oil for frying

Directions

1. Finely chop onion and garlic cloves and cook gently in a little oil for a few minutes until soft but not brown.
2. Put the onion mix into a large bowl and add meat, breadcrumbs, savory, and egg yolk.
3. Mix together well with wet hands or use a food processor.
4. Shape into small balls.
5. Heat oil in a pan over medium heat, adding a little more if needed and sear the meatballs all over to brown. They will need to be seared for 5–10 minutes.
6. Remove meatballs from the pan and use in your favorite dish. Either simmer in a tomato and basil sauce and serve with pasta, or in a thickened gravy with peas and diced carrots and serve with mashed potato. Meatballs will need to cook for 10–15 minutes.

SORREL (*Rumex acetosa*)
FRENCH SORREL (*Rumex scutatus*)
(perennial)

There was mention of sorrel in culinary manuscripts from over two thousand years ago, but sorrel hasn't been documented well over the centuries, probably because it grows wild and never needed to be cultivated. It's native to Europe and Asia, but has spread across America and is now a fairly common garden plant in many countries.

French sorrel (*Rumex scutatus*) seems to be the most popular type of sorrel to grow in herb gardens. Sorrel has similar qualities to spinach and can be prepared and eaten in the same way. French sorrel, as the name suggests, is used in many French recipes as well as being a popular "pot herb." Both types of sorrel are used medicinally, as well as in the kitchen.

The plant can grow to around 4–5' (1–1.5 m) in height and produces flowers throughout the summer months.

GROWING ADVICE

Sorrel can be grown as an annual or a perennial. After a few years, the plants can become coarse and should be replaced. Sorrel can be grown in full sun and does thrive in a sunny spot, but tends to "bolt" or run to seed quickly in hot, dry spells. Either protect your plants from full sun, especially in the hottest part of the day, or plant in a position that will get some shade. Sorrel can be propagated from seed or root division.

From Seed

Seed can be sown directly in the garden from late spring to early summer. Dig over the bed quite deeply and remove any perennial weeds. Rake to a fine consistency. Sow seeds about 1" (2.5 cm) deep in rows around 18" (46 cm) apart. Keep watered, but not too wet.

When the seedlings are large enough to handle, thin to allow the stronger plants space to grow, approximately 10–12" (25.5–30.5 cm). Because sorrel grows in clumps, a spacing of around 12" (30.5 cm) is usually recommended, but if the soil is dug deeply or if you're using a raised bed system, sorrel can be grown closer together.

Seeds can also be started early in the year in a greenhouse or conservatory. Sow as early as March, as long as the pots can be kept warm. Sow a few seeds in pots of fresh compost. Make sure the pots are well-drained, but not allowed to dry out.

It's a good idea to use degradable pots to avoid damaging roots when transplanting to the garden. After all danger of frost has passed, transplant the sorrel plants out into their permanent position in the herb garden or in containers.

Root Division

In the autumn, choose a healthy plant and dig up carefully to avoid damaging the roots too much. Divide the root clump into pieces and replant in the garden as soon as possible. Only plant

Aim to dig up sorrel for plant division every three to five years.

out pieces of root that are healthy and free from disease. Water in well after planting.

After a few years, sorrel can get coarse and should be replaced as necessary. Sorrel is often grown as an annual from seed every year. If your sorrel plants start running to seed too early, cut off the flowering stems. The flower stems can be cut off as they appear, unless you want to grow the flowers to use or to allow the plant to seed itself.

If left to its own devices, sorrel can be somewhat invasive in the herb bed, so keep an eye out for plants coming up everywhere if you let them reseed. Sorrel sometimes sends out runners to make new plants. Remove these if you need to contain your sorrel bed. Cut runners from the main plant and dig up the new plants carefully to avoid damaging the roots if you want to replant them. Replant as soon as possible after digging up. When the plants start to grow tall in the summer, cut the stems down and the roots will push up fresh new shoots.

Container Growing

Sorrel is suitable for containers and pots, but pots must be fairly large and well-drained. Water regularly during the growing season and never let the soil dry out. However, pots left out in the winter or during a rainy season can get waterlogged, so it's important to protect from too much rainfall.

Sorrel Soup

This is a quick recipe, but for whatever style of soup you're making, sorrel should be added 5–10 minutes before the end of the cooking time.

Ingredients

- 1 medium or large potato, peeled and cut into small pieces
- ½ cup fresh sorrel
- Oil or butter for sautéing
- 1 small onion, chopped
- 1¼ pints vegetable stock
- Salt and pepper, to taste
- Boiled eggs

For a creamy soup (optional):
- 1 cup milk
- A little cream (optional)

Directions

1. In a large pan, sauté the potato and onion in the oil or butter for a minute or two.
2. Add stock to the pan, stir, and bring to a boil. Reduce heat and simmer for about 15–20 minutes until potato is soft.
3. Add the sorrel and cook for another 5 minutes. Taste and season with salt and pepper.
4. If a creamy soup is desired, pour into a blender and process until smooth. Return to the pan and stir in the milk. Gently bring to a boil, stirring to avoid sticking, and remove from heat immediately.
5. Serve in individual bowls with a swirl of single cream.
6. Top with half a boiled egg for each serving.

HARVESTING AND STORING

Young leaves are best used fresh, but can be dried for use in the winter months or when the plant is resting. Leaves should be dried on racks or hung in small bunches in a dry, airy, and dust-free place until crisp. Crumble into glass jars. Label and store out of direct light.

MEDICINAL USES FOR SORREL

Sorrel contains high levels of oxalic acid and shouldn't be used in medicinal preparations for people suffering with rheumatism.

Sorrel has been used in infusions to treat sore throats.

It is a natural laxative and is often used to treat constipation. Sorrel is also believed to cleanse and purify the body from toxins.

RECIPE IDEAS

Sorrel can be cooked as a green vegetable. Steam gently as you would cook spinach.

TARRAGON (*Artemisia dracunculus*)
(perennial)

Tarragon is native to southern Europe and is now widely grown throughout Europe and elsewhere. Although it's a perennial plant, it's unlikely to produce seed in cooler climates unless it's kept in a warm environment throughout the winter months. It will keep growing, but will need dividing every two or three years, or fresh seed should be sown regularly to ensure a healthy crop.

The true French tarragon isn't always easy to grow from seed and the seed can be hard to find, although small plants may be available from garden suppliers and nurseries. Russian tarragon is slightly coarser but hardier, and is often grown in place of French tarragon.

Tarragon can be grown successfully in containers, but it isn't a particularly decorative plant. It's used extensively in cooking, as well as being added to vinegars and salad dressings. It has a subtle flavor and is often used to enhance dishes. Tarragon is a warming herb and is said to stimulate appetite and lower fevers.

GROWING ADVICE

Tarragon can be started from seed, although it's unusual to find true French tarragon seed. Buy a ready-grown plant from a nursery if the seed is unavailable or find someone who is growing French tarragon and can share a cutting or two. Many gardeners find they have too many plants when it comes to perennials and will happily give some away.

Otherwise, Russian tarragon can be grown from seed and will self-seed in warmer climates, or if protected through cold winter months. Russian tarragon, like the French variety, can be propagated by root division and should be lifted every few years and divided to give the plants a better chance of thriving.

From Seed

Seed is generally sown around April, but check your seed packet for the manufacturer's growing recommendations for your region. Sow the seed

In some countries, there are restrictions on growing plants of the Artemisia family, as well as restrictions on some extracts from these plants.

Tarragon cuttings are the best and easiest method to propagate and grow more.

in well-drained trays or pots of fresh compost and keep out of direct light and indoors.

Keep trays and pots indoors until the seedlings start to appear. The compost should be kept damp, but not too wet. When the seedlings are starting to show, the trays can be put outside during the day. Bring them indoors at night until the air temperature gets a little warmer. When they're large enough to handle, plant out to their permanent positions.

Tarragon also grows well in containers. Position your plants in the herb garden or in containers in a sunny position, if possible, although tarragon will also grow well in partial shade. Dig the ground over before planting and remove any perennial weeds and nonorganic debris. Rake to a fine consistency and water plants straight after planting. Keep weeds away and the ground fairly damp, but not too wet.

From Cuttings

This is probably the best way to get French tarragon going in your herb garden. Take 3–4" (7.5–10 cm) cuttings from established plants in the spring and push cut end of stems into pots of fresh compost. If you have space in the seed bed, tarragon cuttings can be planted directly outside,

although they should be protected at night with a cloche during the winter months.

Keep watered during dry weather and plant out the following year when the cuttings have developed roots. Both Russian and French tarragon can be propagated from cuttings.

Root Division

Roots can be divided in the spring or autumn. Choose a well-established and healthy plant and dig up carefully to avoid damaging the roots too much. Divide the roots into several pieces and replant straight away in a sunny or semi-shady position. Water well and keep weeds away. Resist picking leaves until the new plants have started growing again.

HARVESTING AND STORING

Tarragon is best used fresh, and some varieties are evergreen so the leaves should be available all year-round. However, sprigs of tarragon can be frozen. Pick in the summer when the plant is at its peak and freeze quickly.

Leaves can also be dried by laying on trays or hanging in bunches in a dry, airy, dust-free place

Container Growing

French tarragon isn't as hardy as the Russian variety and is suited to growing in pots and containers. They should be wide, deep, and well-drained. Fill with a good organic compost, don't over-water, and keep in a sunny place. Protect plants by bringing them indoors in cold weather.

Tarragon Chicken

Tarragon and chicken pair extremely well together, as the herb isn't overpowering.
(Serves 2)

Ingredients

- 4 chicken thighs
- 2–3 cloves garlic, sliced lengthwise
- 1 small/medium onion, chopped; or 2 shallots, sliced
- ½–¾ cup quartered mushrooms
- 2 teaspoons Dijon mustard
- ¾–1 cup chicken stock
- 1–2 tablespoons finely chopped tarragon leaves
- ¼–⅓ cup heavy or whipping cream
- Salt and freshly ground black pepper, to taste
- Cooking oil
- 4 strips smoked streaky bacon, rind removed and sliced into small pieces (optional)

Directions

1. In a large casserole-type pan, heat a couple of tablespoons of cooking oil over medium heat.
2. Season the chicken with salt and pepper and fry until golden brown on each side. Remove from the pan and set aside.
3. Add a little more oil to the pan, then add the garlic, chopped onion or sliced shallots, and bacon, if using. Stir over medium heat until the onions or shallots have started to soften and, if using, the bacon has started to change color.
4. Add the mushrooms to the pan and continue frying for a minute or two.
5. Add the chicken stock, mustard, and about ⅔ of the tarragon.
6. Put the chicken back into the pan and bring to a simmer. Cook gently for about 20 minutes or until the chicken is cooked through.
7. Stir in the cream, bring back to simmering, and cook for another 2 minutes with the lid off the pan.
8. Season with salt and pepper and serve, scattering the remaining tarragon over the whole dish.

out of direct light. When leaves are fully dry, store in glass jars and label. Keep all dried herbs out of direct light to reduce loss of flavor.

MEDICINAL USES FOR TARRAGON

Tarragon isn't used in medicinal preparations these days, although it was once used to treat toothaches. However, it's a warming herb and can help reduce fevers.

Tarragon also encourages appetite, but is predominantly a culinary herb.

RECIPE IDEAS

Tarragon is often used to flavor chicken, but will enhance vegetarian dishes just as well.

THYME (*Thymus vulgaris*)
(perennial)

Thyme is a hardy perennial and will last in your herb garden for several years. It's easily propagated and has been cultivated in kitchen gardens for centuries. Originating from Mediterranean areas, it will tolerate dry conditions. There are several myths and legends attached to thyme, proving that over the centuries, it has always played an important part in everyday life. For example, it was once believed if a woman wore thyme in her hair, she would attract a husband.

Thyme has been used in food preparation and in the preserving of meat since Roman times. It has also been the main ingredient in many medicinal preparations and is known to soothe coughs and colds, as well as cure a number of minor ailments.

Thyme is certainly sweet smelling and is invaluable in a kitchen. It should be added early in cooking because it's slow to release its flavors. There are a number of varieties of thyme, but the garden thyme (*Thymus vulgaris*) and the lemon-scented thyme (*Thymus citriodorus*) exceed most other types for taste and aroma.

GROWING ADVICE

Thyme can be started from seed, cuttings, or root division. Once your plants are established, use as much as you can. It's a useful herb, both medicinally and in the kitchen. Cut short stems and rub the leaves off with a blunt knife or your finger.

From Seed

Sowing your own seed is very satisfying, but it will be a while before you can use the leaves. Sow seed in early spring in well-drained trays or pots of seed compost and plant outside later in the year when the plants are strong enough. Check your seed packet for growing recommendations.

Thyme seed can be directly sown into the garden around early to mid-spring, as long as all danger of frost has passed. Sow in shallow drills about 12" (30.5 cm) apart and water. Keep weed-free and watered until germination, but be careful to not over-water thyme. While it prefers a dry environment, the seed will need some water to germinate.

Thin the young plants as they come up, leaving space for the others to grow. Thyme likes space and makes a good ground cover for small patches in the garden. The plants removed from the line can be replanted or potted up.

Don't use any leaves in the first year of growth. Let the plant become established and produce strong roots first.

Thyme should be placed in a sunny and dry place in the garden, if possible. It's happy to grow in containers and will thrive near a rockery, raised herb garden, or on a stone wall. The soil must be well-drained. Water occasionally, but never let the ground become too wet. Thyme also likes a light soil. If your soil is heavy, mix some sand in before planting.

Root Division

Thyme needs to be divided every three or four years when the plant becomes woody and straggly. Dig up carefully and pull the roots apart. Choose the healthiest pieces and replant around the garden or in pots. Thyme potted up in a pretty container makes a lovely gift.

Cuttings

To grow thyme from cuttings, cut fresh stems from an established, healthy plant in the spring. Push the cuttings into potting compost and water. Before planting, dip cut ends in hormone gel or powder, if available. Keep the pots in

Container Growing

Such an attractive plant deserves its own special place in the garden and will thrive in a well-drained container or large pot on a patio or balcony. Thyme will also grow on a kitchen windowsill, given enough sunlight and water. Although this herb will tolerate near drought conditions, when growing in pots, it should be watered from time to time, especially in dry weather periods or if grown indoors. Repot every two or three years and treat to an organic feed every now and then. If a very cold winter is expected, plants can be brought inside, or apply mulch to protect the roots during the winter months.

a warm, sunny place, preferably indoors, or sheltered from cold and wind if outside. Water occasionally, but don't let the soil become too wet, and make sure the pots are well-drained. Plant out cuttings that have developed roots and are starting to grow more leaves the following year. In very cold winters where temperatures drop to 10°F or below, a mulch will help protect the roots from freezing.

Thyme can be started from cuttings.

Perfect Thyme Roasties

Roasties are simply roasted potatoes that have the perfect level of fluff on the inside and crisp on the outside.

Ingredients

- Potatoes
- 2–4 sprigs fresh thyme
- Salt and black pepper, to taste
- 1–2 tablespoons duck or goose fat

Directions

1. Prepare the potatoes: peel and cut into evenly sized pieces. Wash to remove some of the starch.
2. Place in a medium to large pan and cover with cold water.
3. Bring to a boil. Lower heat a little and simmer for 10–15 minutes until nearly cooked. Turn on the oven and preheat to 390°F (199°C).
4. Drain and shake potatoes in a colander to roughen edges slightly and to remove excess water.
5. Return potatoes to dry pan and stir in the duck or goose fat.
6. Strip leaves from thyme sprigs and stir into the potatoes, adding a little salt and black pepper to season.
7. Put potatoes on a baking tray and cook in preheated oven until crispy and cooked through, about 15–35 minutes, depending on the size of potato pieces.

HARVESTING AND STORING

Pick leaves and stems when the plant is established and stems are at least 8" (20 cm) long. Thyme is better used fresh, but can be dried by hanging stems upside down in paper bags, or laying on trays in a dark and airy place until the leaves can be crumbled. Store in a sealed jar and label. Keep out of direct light. Stems can be frozen as well. Pick when the flowers are starting to appear and freeze quickly.

MEDICINAL USES FOR THYME

Thyme is well-known for alleviating common cold symptoms, taken usually as a tisane.

It's also a natural antiseptic and is a good, quick cure for cuts and scrapes in the garden.

RECIPE IDEAS

Thyme is a wonderful flavoring herb, and a thyme and lemon tea can help prevent colds. Pour boiled water in a jug over a sprig or two of thyme and add a slice of lemon or lemon juice. Let it steep for 5 minutes, strain, and serve. Add a spoonful of honey for an extra healthy boost and a sweeter taste.

VIOLETS (*Viola odorata*)
(perennial)

Viola odorata is the species known as "sweet violets." The smell and taste live up to their reputation. Sweet violet flowers are candied and used in many cakes and other confections. They have a unique smell and taste and can't be forgotten once tried.

Violets are a woodland plant and if left to grow, make an excellent ground cover, growing to around 3–4" (7.5–10 cm) in height. The leaves can be used to thicken stews and are also added to salads. The delicate flowers normally bloom in late winter and early spring, making it one of the first colorful plants of the year. Violet flowers have a very delicate yet unmistakable scent are used in confectionary, and infused in a tisane.

Violets belong to the *Viola* family of which there are hundreds of types, although it's the *Viola odorata* that is most commonly used as an herb. The plants will grow in sunny positions, as they're quite hardy and adaptable, but the ground must be kept watered in dry periods. They are happiest in semi-shade and are often found growing wild in light, woodland areas.

GROWING ADVICE

Violets are best propagated from established plants, and they develop new plants from the roots. They can also be started from seed. Violet flowers are perfect for visiting bees, but usually bloom before the bees are out and about, so they aren't often pollinated and rarely produce seed.

Violets sometimes flower again in autumn, but the flower, although full of seed, isn't attractive to bees at that time, so again, doesn't get pollinated. Sowing violets from seed can be erratic and it's usually best to propagate by division of the plants, or detaching small plants from the runners produced from the main plant.

Violets are a woodland plant and will thrive in semi shade, but as long as the ground doesn't dry out, they are happy to grow in a sunny position.

From Seed

If you do want to try your hand at propagating sweet violets from seed, start by buying a packet of seeds from a reputable seed company and check the manufacturer's growing recommendations for

Violets have been used since at least 500 BC as a medicinal herb.

Violets growing wild in nature.

Root Division

In the autumn, plants can be gently lifted and divided into two or more pieces. Dig carefully around the plants to avoid damaging the roots, then replant the undamaged and healthy pieces. Plant out in well-drained pots or containers and transplant into the garden during the following spring or autumn when they're growing well.

Cuttings

Violets can also be started from cuttings taken from healthy plants in the autumn. Push cuttings into well-drained pots of fresh compost and water. If available, dip cut ends in hormone gel or powder before planting. Look after them during the winter months and plant out the following autumn when the cuttings have developed roots and are starting to grow.

Violet plants are evergreen, and the leaves can be used all year-round. Young leaves are best used in salads, and the larger leaves, produced later in the year, are good to add to soups and stews, as they have a thickening effect. The flowers should be picked and used as available. Add to salads or use to flavor sweet dishes. Flowers are often candied and used as decoration for fancy cakes.

your region before you start. Generally, the seed should be planted early in the spring and kept in a warm place. Sow in well-drained pots or trays of fresh compost and keep damp, but not too wet. Seeds may take some time to germinate. Although violets can tolerate very low temperatures, they should be kept indoors until the outside temperature is warm if starting from seed. When the seedlings are large enough to handle and all danger of frost has passed, either repot or plant outside in their permanent positions. Allow about 12" (30.5 cm) of growing space per plant.

From Runners

In spring or autumn, cut the runner from the main plant and transplant to its new position, if necessary, in full sun or semi-shade. Water plants well after transplanting and firm down carefully with your heel.

Container Growing

Violets grow well in containers, which should be well-drained and 4" (10 cm) deep and 6–8" (15–20 cm) wide. Plants like cool weather and should be moved into a shady spot during sunny days. Water when the top inch of soil is dry.

Flowery Snack

This recipe is simply a delicious avocado spread on your preferred toasted bread, garnished with edible flowers.

Ingredients

- Slices of bread
- Avocado paste
- Violet flowers
- Daisy flowers
- Light chili flakes or preferred seasoning

Directions

1. Spread avocado paste over slices of bread.
2. Sprinkle over chili flakes or other seasoning.
3. Top with violet and daisy blooms.

Variation

Lightly butter bread and arrange thin slices of fresh avocado on top. Add as many violet flowers as you like.

HARVESTING AND STORING

Leaves are evergreen and shouldn't need storing, but can be dried if necessary. Dry by hanging in small bunches in a dark, airy place until crisp, then crumble into glass jars and label. Store out of direct light. Flowers can be dried for making tea and candied for decorating cakes and desserts.

MEDICINAL USES FOR VIOLETS

Many conditions have been treated with violets. In recent years, fresh leaves have been found to help in curing some cancers. The leaves have expectorant properties, making it good for alleviating bronchial conditions. It's also a mild laxative and should not be taken in large doses. Violets are used in herbal preparations worldwide and have been for many centuries.

RECIPE IDEAS

Violets can be steeped to make a delicious tea, but to get the best flavor and color, pour boiling water over violet blooms in a jug and leave overnight. Strain into cups and add a spoonful of honey, then top with boiling hot water.

Violets are often candied and used in cake decoration. The leaves and flowers are edible and the flowers will brighten up the greenest of salads.

WATERCRESS (*Nasturtium officinale*)
(perennial)

Watercress is one of the few herbs you can grow that really does like its roots in water. The herb originated in Europe and Asia, but is now grown in many countries. Traditionally grown in streams of running water, watercress can often be found growing wild, although care should be taken when collecting from the wild. The water source could be contaminated with animal droppings or agricultural chemicals, which may not affect the taste of the plant, but it will affect its properties and can cause illness.

Watercress has been used as a medicinal and culinary herb for over two thousand years and is considered a "super food" for almost as long and became a commercial product in the early nineteenth century. By the early twentieth century, watercress had developed into a large business with London being the heart of the watercress trading world.

For many years, it has been used to encourage growth in children and keep soldiers strong and prepared for battle. The herb contains, gram for gram, as much vitamin C as oranges, as much calcium as milk, and also vast quantities of potassium and iron, making the folklore about watercress being a super food quite accurate. There are so many minerals and vitamins in watercress that eating a bunch a day would probably cancel out any need for vitamin supplements.

GROWING ADVICE

It has, until recently, been thought impossible to grow watercress without a pure spring water source. However, watercress can be grown in an old paddling pool if conditions are good. If you do happen to have a pure spring water source, so much the better.

From Seed

If you want to grow cress in a regular vegetable bed, you will need to buy seeds of a land cress variety. Check on the packet for manufacturer's growing instructions before you buy. There are a number of ways to get cress going and seed is readily available from garden suppliers.

Watercress isn't a true water plant, as the plant grows above water and has only its roots beneath the surface.

Seed can be sown in a seed tray of very moist compost, but the tray or pot should be

A small garden pond is the perfect place to cultivate watercress.

well-drained and watered regularly. The seed won't germinate in dry conditions or in stagnant water. When the plants are large enough to handle, plant them out in their permanent position. If watercress gets well-established in your garden, it can become invasive, but harvesting regularly should help overcome this. If left to grow, watercress can grow to over 3' (1 m) in length, but shoots are normally cut at around 8" (20 cm) or so.

Plants can be placed in a clean and cool garden pond. The pond must be cleaned regularly or have a running water source pumped through it. Watercress will also survive on the banks of a stream if moist enough. It's also not a particular sun lover and will do well in very cool water and partial shade.

Watercress can also be grown at home in an old paddling pool, full of soil. Make sure the pool is well-drained and watered regularly. Containers must be well-drained, so the water doesn't become stagnant. Watercress ideally thrives in pure spring water.

From Cuttings

If you buy watercress from your local produce store in bunches, the stems will sometimes take root. Place a few healthy stems in a glass of water and change the water often. The cuttings that develop roots can be planted out later, or source a few plants or cuttings from a local grower.

Never let the roots dry out, keep the water clean, and you should be able to produce a steady crop of this wonderful plant all year-round. In the winter months, watercress is coarser, but can be added to soups and stews instead of eaten raw in salads.

Container Growing

Watercress should be contained, although not necessarily in the usual way with ceramic pots and decorative troughs. Plants are best grown in ponds, streams, and children's pools and as previously mentioned, need a constant water supply or to be watered regularly. They also need good drainage if planted in compost or soil. Poorly growing plants are usually suffering from waterlogging in stagnant water.

Watercress Soup

Raw watercress has a fresh, bitter, and peppery flavor that can be compared to mustard greens or wasabi, but when cooked, its flavor mellows out a bit.

Ingredients

- 1–1¼ cups roughly chopped watercress
- 1 cup peeled and diced potatoes
- 1 small/medium onion, chopped
- 1 small stick celery, chopped into small pieces (optional)
- 3 tablespoons butter
- 2½ cups vegetable or chicken stock
- ⅔ cup milk
- Salt and black pepper, to taste

Directions

1. Put the butter in a large pan and gently heat until just melted, but not browned.
2. Add chopped onion and stir over low heat until onion has started to soften. Stir in the celery and cook for another minute or two.
3. Add diced potatoes and stock to the pan. Stir and bring to a boil over a medium to high heat. Lower heat and simmer for 15 minutes, or until potatoes and celery are soft.
4. Stir in the watercress and cook for another 5 minutes.
5. Mix soup in a blender or food processor until smooth. Return to a clean pan.
6. Stir in the milk and seasoning to taste and reheat until piping hot.

Harvest watercress often and cut straggly stems. When you cut watercress, the roots develop more shoots and the plants become stronger, so don't forget to use it.

Read the growing recommendations on seed packets before you buy, as this is a plant that requires unique cultivation techniques, so it's best to choose a specific variety for your region and available space.

HARVESTING AND STORING

Watercress can be stored in a glass of water in a cold place, preferably a fridge, for a couple of days. Place cut end down in an inch or two of fresh cold water. As watercress will often produce fresh shoots year-round, it's not usually necessary to store it.

MEDICINAL USES FOR WATERCRESS

Watercress has been used to treat many illnesses and medical conditions, too numerable to mention.

Because of its high vitamin and mineral content—including folic acid, which is relatively scarce in plant life—watercress is a natural tonic and will help the body repair itself.

Eating a couple of handfuls of watercress every day will give the immune system a boost and help stave off colds and flu.

RECIPE IDEAS

Add chopped watercress to salads and casseroles. Don't overcook it. Add it to a stew or casserole during the last few minutes of cooking.

YARROW (*Achillea millefolium*)
(perennial)

Yarrow has long been associated with divination and can be found in the *I Ching* or *Book of Changes*. It also has a long medicinal history and is considered to be one of the most effective healing herbs for centuries.

Yarrow has been used in culinary and cosmetic preparations, is an effective medicinal herb, and can be a substitute for hops in brewing beer. Yarrow is still used today in home preparations and in Ayurvedic medicine, often employed as a tonic. Prolonged use, however, can cause allergic reactions.

Yarrow is native to Europe, but is now fairly widespread over moderate climates and grows wild in meadows, pastures, and along the roadside. It will always be found growing in a sunny position and often in fairly poor soil. Cultivating yarrow in the herb garden has to be carefully controlled, as it can become invasive. Yarrow is a useful herb for repelling beetles and ants, and a plant or two in the vegetable garden will repel pests. A yarrow plant in a container near the entrance to a house will repel flies.

GROWING ADVICE

Don't plant yarrow in a richly composted area of the garden. It doesn't thrive in a rich soil and will often do much better in poor soil conditions, as long as it's in full sun. Yarrow can grow up to 2' (61 cm) tall and needs a sunny position to grow well.

It can be planted alongside pathways where the soil hasn't been cultivated, or next to the back door to prevent bugs from entering the house. It can be propagated from seed or by division.

Yarrow is very suitable for container growing, as it tolerates drying out occasionally.

From Seed

Yarrow likes a light soil and a sunny position. If your soil is too heavy, dig in some sand or light gravel to add drainage. Sow seed in the spring in well-drained trays or pots of fresh compost. Yarrow can be sown directly in a seed bed and protected from cold nights with a cloche or in a cold frame. In some regions, certain varieties of seed can be sown in the autumn. Check the

Yarrow seeds can take months to germinate.

Container Growing

Yarrow grows well in containers, although they should be well-drained and fairly large. A pot holding 1 gallon will suffice. Water in hot weather, but never allow pots to become waterlogged. If you're growing a tall variety, it may be necessary to support the plants. Place canes or other supports before planting as to not damage the roots.

manufacturer's growing recommendations on your seed packet for your region before sowing.

Water the seeds, but never let the soil become waterlogged or too wet. Seed can take up to three months to germinate. When the seedlings are large enough to handle, they can be pricked out into individual pots or, if the ground and air temperatures are warm enough, planted directly into the garden. Although yarrow is a hardy plant and fairly frost tolerant, the seedlings will need protecting from bad weather until they're established.

Root Division

In the autumn, plants can be divided if necessary. Using a fork, dig carefully around a well-established healthy plant and divide into two or more pieces, depending on the size of the root structure. Replant the divided pieces straight away and heel down carefully. Water in well and mulch in the winter if the ground is likely to become frozen. Yarrow doesn't like too much moisture, so be careful not to mulch too heavily. Don't mulch at all if the ground is very wet.

From Cuttings

Yarrow can also be started from cuttings taken in spring or autumn. Push 3–4" (7.5–10 cm) cuttings dipped in hormone gel or powder, if available, into pots of fresh compost and gently water. Keep in a sunny spot and water regularly. Always position yarrow in a well-drained and sunny place.

Harvest flowers and leaves as they become available. Young leaves can be added to salads, although they're rather bitter. Flowers are often made into tisanes.

Be careful yarrow doesn't take over. You may have to pull out a few plants every year to allow the other plants in the garden to breathe. Although, if you harvest all the flowers, they won't have a chance to reseed.

The common name "woundwort" confirms that yarrow was used to heal wounds, and it's also been helpful for stemming nosebleeds and for treating more serious wounds.

Yarrow Omelet

This healthy breakfast is an excellent way to use some of your homegrown yarrow! (Makes 2 servings)

Ingredients

- 4–6 eggs
- 1 tablespoon chopped yarrow, or to taste
- Oil, for frying
- Salt and pepper, to taste
- Grated cheese (optional)
- Grated onion (optional)

Directions

1. Beat eggs in a large bowl until mixed well and bubbly.
2. Stir in the chopped yarrow and salt and pepper.
3. Heat oil in a frying pan.
4. Pour egg mixture into the pan and sprinkle grated cheese and onion over the eggs, if using.
5. Gently cook the omelet to your preference. Either turn the whole thing over after about 5 minutes or set under a medium-hot grill.
6. Serve hot.

Note: This recipe is for a basic omelet, but feel free to be adventurous and mix in any other ingredients of your choice; tomatoes, cooked bacon, peppers, etc.

HARVESTING AND STORING

Leaves and flowers can be dried. Hang stems upside down in paper bags in an airy place until completely dry. Store in glass jars, label, and keep out of direct light. The whole herb—leaves and flowers—can be used to make tea and medicinal preparations. The flowers also make a nice, dried flower arrangement.

MEDICINAL USES FOR YARROW

A compress can be made from yarrow to assist the healing of wounds.

Tea made from fresh leaves is often successful in alleviating cold and flu symptoms.

Yarrow has been used medicinally for centuries. It's still used today in herbal remedies treating kidney disorders, menstrual pain, and other conditions. However, it can be harmful if taken regularly over a long period of time.

A stem of yarrow thrown on the barbeque after cooking will repel mosquitoes.

RECIPE IDEAS

Yarrow tends to be used mostly as a tea and should be steeped in hot water for about 5 minutes, strained, and served. But yarrow can also be added to stews or fresh in salads. All parts of the plant are edible.

Spices

The ancient spice trade—in which herbs, drugs, and spices were caravanned or shipped around the world—was filled with romance and mystery. The origins of some spices were kept secret, allowing traders to charge extraordinary prices for these sought-after products. Today, however, we have the information necessary to grow these wonderful plants at home. Knowing where the plants originate is crucial to getting their growing conditions right.

CARAWAY (*Carum carvi*)
(*biennial*)

Caraway tends to be underrated as a garden herb. Although it's native to many regions, including Europe and Asia, it's only commercially grown in a few places and then mostly for the seed. The leaves and roots of caraway are also edible, and it has been said that caraway roots, which are slightly smaller than parsnips, are tastier than many root vegetables. The leaves can be used in salads and soups and taste similar to dill. Records of caraway being used as a medicinal and culinary herb go back thousands of years.

Caraway is in the same family as parsley and grows about 12" (30.5 cm) tall in the first year and then up to 2' (61 cm) in the second year before it produces seed. It's often found growing on wasteland. An easy herb to grow, although it can become slightly invasive, caraway is an excellent choice for an herb garden.

GROWING ADVICE

Garden suppliers don't always stock ready-grown caraway plants, although it's possible to find them.

The best way to start your herbs is by sowing seed. Seed should be started directly in the prepared bed, as caraway has tap roots and doesn't transplant well. Choose a sunny, well-drained spot and dig the ground over well. Dig fairly deep, especially if you want the roots to grow to full maturity. Remove any nonorganic debris, large stones, and perennial weeds to give the plants a good start.

Make sure the soil is fairly light. Caraway has a long tap root and growth will be stunted in heavy clay soils. Dig in some sand if necessary. Rake the surface over to a fine consistency and sow the seed in lines about 12" (30.5 cm) apart. Cover with very little soil and water gently. Keep weed-free and watered. Caraway tends to germinate easily.

Seed can be sown in spring or late summer to autumn. Spring sowings will flower the following year, but the leaf is available for use throughout the first year. Autumn sowings will flower in late summer the following year. Autumn sowings from seed recently ripened often germinate better than seed kept until the following spring. However, if

Because caraway plants can be hard to find, growing from seed is usually the best way to cultivate in your garden.

the winter is likely to be cold in your region, it's advisable to protect the seedlings over the winter months with a cloche or cold frame.

Caraway has delicate, lacy foliage, but can sometimes be mistaken for a weed. Generally, it won't grow to more than 12" (30.5 cm) during the first year and weeds tend to grow taller. Hoe gently from time to time to remove any weeds. When the plants are large enough to handle, they should be thinned out to allow about 8" (20 cm) between each plant.

As the plant grows, leaves can be picked regularly. This will help develop more root growth. During the second year of growth, caraway will produce less foliage, but will grow flowers from which the seed is collected. When the flower heads start to dry, remove them from the plant. If caraway is allowed to self-seed, it can become invasive in the herb garden, so picking off all the flowers will solve the problem.

During very cold winters, mulch the plants to prevent damage to the roots. After the flowers have died and been removed during the second year, the root can be dug up and eaten as a vegetable, similar to parsnip.

Generally, caraway is a fairly hardy plant, but is occasionally attacked by caterpillars.

Container Growing

Caraway can become invasive in the garden in milder climates; therefore, it makes an ideal candidate for container growing. However, because of the long tap root, the containers will need to be very deep and well-draining. If these conditions are met, then caraway should grow very happily in a container. Barrel-shaped containers full of caraway with their feathery, very decorative foliage make attractive patio planters.

HARVESTING AND STORING

When flowers are dying, remove from the plant and hang upside down in paper bags to collect the seed. Store seed in a dark glass jar, as light will weaken them. Use them in cakes, bread, and other dishes.

Leaves are not suitable for storing, although young leaves could be hung until crisp enough to crumble. Use as a flavoring in winter soups. Roots are best eaten directly after harvesting, but should keep for a couple of days in the fridge.

MEDICINAL USES FOR CARAWAY

Although caraway was once considered to be a retaining medication for keeping your loved one, it's used chiefly as a flavoring these days.

The essential oil of caraway is known to reduce flatulence and is a mild tonic. It is often used with other medications.

RECIPE IDEAS

Caraway is one of the herbs that can be used in sweet or savory dishes. The seed has been traditionally used to flavor bread and cakes, as well as pickles, cabbage, cauliflower, and cheese.

CHILI PEPPERS (*Capsicum annuum*)
(*perennial*)

Although chili pepper plants are perennial, they're usually grown as annual plants in moderate and cooler climates. Chili peppers are native to warmer climates, but they grow remarkably well in cooler regions. They're in the same family as sweet peppers and need more or less the same growing conditions.

There is archaeological evidence of wild peppers being cultivated for human consumption as far back as 5000 BC. Chili peppers were thought, for centuries, to have originated in India, but they actually came from South America. By the late sixteenth century, peppers were used in all regions of the world, especially in Europe and India.

You will probably only need a few chili pepper plants as they produce many fruits, as opposed to sweet pepper plants, which will produce fewer fruits. There are many different varieties of peppers, and they come in all shapes, colors, and sizes. Decide on what you and your family will eat. If you don't use hot spices in your food very often, just grow one or two chili pepper plants for when you do need them.

GROWING ADVICE

Generally, chili peppers should be treated the same as sweet peppers, although they can be less tolerant of cold weather, so check on the manufacturer's recommended sowing times on the seed packet for your particular region.

From Seed

Start seed in well-drained trays or pots of fresh potting or seed compost. Keep warm and watered until seedlings appear and are large enough to handle. When they have three or four true leaves, repot into individual pots or plant out in the herb bed or vegetable patch.

Make sure all danger of frost has passed and the soil and air temperatures have warmed up. Although they may tolerate some cold, a frost or huge temperature drop could kill very young plants.

Planting On

Dig over the soil in a sunny well-drained spot, remove any weeds and large stones, and rake or

Chilis are also believed to ward off evil in some cultures and are hung with a lemon over a doorway into the house.

hoe to a fairly fine consistency. Dip the pots in water before you remove the plants to limit root damage and gently but firmly plant out in rows or around the garden. Allow at least 18" (46 cm) of space for each plant to grow into.

Chili plants can help deter bugs from vegetable crops, so it's a good idea to grow a plant or two in your vegetable garden. Keep plants weed-free and make sure they get enough water in dry periods. Chili peppers will thrive in a sunny spot in the garden, however, if the leaves start wilting, they may be getting too much sun.

Provide shade during the hottest part of the day, but remember to remove the shade later. Use chili peppers as and when they become available. Check the seed packet for maturity patterns. They can often be eaten green or left until red. In cooler climates, sweet peppers don't always reach the

Even if you don't like hot spice, it's a good idea to grow chili plants in your garden because they will help protect your other vegetable crops from bugs.

Container Growing

Chili pepper plants are attractive and ideally suited to container growing. Fill well-drained pots with fresh compost and plant seedlings or young plants firmly, taking care to handle stems and roots as little as possible. Water well after planting. Keep a plant or two in a large pot or container in a sunny spot in the house, or on a patio or balcony. Chilis are also a great plant to grow in a greenhouse, as they can deter bugs from your other crops. Keep out of cold drafts and remember to water them.

red stage, but chili peppers are smaller and ripen more quickly.

Sometimes picking early chilis will encourage the plant to produce more fruits, although not all varieties or regions will allow this, so check the seed manufacturer's recommended growing instructions for your region and variety before picking off early fruits.

HARVESTING AND STORING

Chilis can be used fresh, but they are often dried. Leave to ripen on the plant and remove in dry weather. Keep in a dark, airy place until dried completely. Store in labeled glass jars out of direct light to avoid loss of flavor and color. Peppers can also be strung up like mushrooms over a warm range or radiator, although care should be taken that they don't collect dust.

Chili con carne is the perfect option to use your own chili peppers and personalize the level of spice.

MEDICINAL USES FOR CHILI PEPPERS

Chili peppers have been cultivated for thousands of years and are not only a very popular spicy addition to food, but they're high in nutritional value. With significant amounts of C, A, and B vitamins, chilis are also a good source of potassium and iron. The high vitamin C content make chilis a practical addition to beans, pulses, and foods that are somewhat lower in vitamin C.

RECIPE IDEAS

Use chili peppers in all recipes that demand a spicy taste. The obvious choice would be to add some to a chili con carne dish. Finely chop before using and avoid using seeds if you prefer a milder taste.

Add fresh or dried chili peppers to stir fries. Remove seeds to avoid overpowering other stir fry ingredients.

Always wash your hands thoroughly after handling chili peppers, especially the seeds, which are the hottest part of the pepper. Don't touch your eyes or mouth before washing your hands.

Larger chili pepper varieties can be used, such as bell (or sweet) peppers. Check taste before using, though; they may be hotter than you expect. Halve and remove seeds, then fill with a mixture of finely chopped zucchini, mushrooms, onion or shallots, and a few halved olives, if available. Top with grated cheese and bake in the oven at 350°F for about 25–30 minutes.

FENUGREEK (*Trigonella foenum-graecum*)
(annual)

Native to Asia and the Mediterranean, fenugreek has grown wild and in cultivation over most of the world for centuries. Fenugreek belongs to the pea family, and is best known for its spicy seed that's used in many different dishes, especially in Indian cuisine. The seeds can be used fresh or roasted, as a coffee substitute, or a powdered spice. Sprouting seeds can also be eaten—simply add them to salads. The seed can provide a useful yellow dye. Leaves from the fenugreek plant are also edible and can be added to curry dishes.

Fenugreek is employed as a fodder crop and has in the past been used in many medicinal preparations. It's now mostly used in Ayurvedic and other alternative therapy medications.

GROWING ADVICE

In tropical climates, fenugreek plants will complete their growth cycle in as little as sixteen weeks, however, in cooler climates this may take about four weeks longer. The plant prefers a warmer climate, so growing in a warm greenhouse or conservatory is advisable if you live in a cooler region. Buy your seed from a reputable company and check on the manufacturer's growing recommendations before you start. Growers recommend soaking the seed in water for about twelve hours before sowing.

Sow seed *in situ* in the spring, or as soon as the temperature has risen significantly after the winter. Choose a sunny spot in the garden and dig over the ground removing large stones and perennial weeds. Hoe or rake to a fine consistency. Make sure the area is well-drained, as roots will rot quickly in waterlogged soil. Keep weed-free and watered in very dry weather.

Sow seeds by scattering thinly and cover with only about half a centimeter of soil. Fenugreek seeds don't like to be buried deep. Make sure they're covered, though, or the birds will find

them before they get a chance to germinate. Water gently with a spray or watering can with rosette attachment to avoid washing the topsoil off the seeds. Seeds normally germinate in a couple of days.

Growing On

When plants are a few inches tall, they should be thinned to allow at least 5–6" (13–15 cm) of growing room per plant. Do this on a wet day to avoid damaging the roots of your small plants. Water the area if the ground is too dry. Fenugreek enjoys fertile soil and a regular organic feed or added compost during the growing season will help your plants thrive.

In cooler climates, sow fenugreek seed in a greenhouse and make sure the soil doesn't dry out. Plants should be thinned out when they're a few inches tall. Keep the soil watered throughout the season, as plants can dry out quickly when they don't have direct rainfall.

If you're growing fenugreek for the shoots, they should be ready to harvest in a few weeks, usually

Container Growing

Large, fairly deep pots or containers should be used for fenugreek. Make sure they're well-drained and fill with fresh, organic compost. Feed plants regularly during the growing season. Pots and containers are good to use in cooler climates, as they can be moved to catch the sunniest spots or brought indoors when the nights get too cold. Don't let compost dry out, but never over-water; creating a near-tropical environment will encourage your plants to thrive.

when they're about 6" (15 cm) tall. Cut at ground level or pull up by the roots. To grow for the seeds, wait for the pods to grow and turn yellow before harvesting. When the plants have died back completely, cut the plant down at ground level

Fenugreek seeds have many health benefits, from aiding digestion to managing blood sugar.

Sprouting Seeds

Fenugreek seed can be "sprouted" like many other plant seeds in a glass jar.

Ingredients

- Fenugreek seeds
- Water
- A large glass jar
- A square of muslin
- An elastic band

Directions

1. Pour a thin layer of seeds into the jar and add tepid water over the seeds, swishing them around for a few seconds to soak thoroughly.
2. Cover the jar with a piece of muslin and secure with an elastic band.
3. Drain all the water through the muslin, then keep the jar in a warm, dark cupboard.
4. Repeat the watering process in the morning and evening. Seeds should start to sprout in 2 or 3 days. Eat when they are 1" (2.5 cm) long.

leaving the roots in the ground. Fenugreek roots, like all plants in the pea family, contain useful nitrogen for the soil. The roots will decompose, and the extra nutrients will benefit your crops next season.

HARVESTING AND STORING

When the pods have ripened on the plants, remove and let them dry out in the sun or in a bright spot indoors for a few hours. Then, either store the whole pods in labeled jars and keep out of direct light, or remove the seeds first and store in the same way. Seeds must be completely dry before storing.

MEDICINAL USES FOR FENUGREEK

Although fenugreek hasn't got medicinal approval yet, it has been shown to alleviate symptoms of various health conditions. Recent research has shown that a controlled amount of powdered fenugreek seed has helped in reducing blood sugar levels and could therefore help reduce the risk of diabetes and heart and blood pressure issues. Always consult your doctor before self-medicating.

Research has shown that large amounts of ground fenugreek seed is detrimental to your health and seed should therefore be taken in small doses in food or as a supplement.

RECIPE IDEAS

Fenugreek can be used in many recipes. Dried seeds can be used fresh or roasted, but they're strong in taste and should be used in moderation.

Add to homemade stews, curries, soups, and breads. Roasted fenugreek seeds can be used as a coffee substitute, but as mentioned above, fenugreek seed shouldn't be consumed in large doses.

Leaves from the fenugreek plant are also edible and can be added to curry dishes.

GARLIC (*Allium sativum*)
(perennial or biennial, often cultivated as an annual)

Garlic is part of the large group of plants belonging to the onion family and was cultivated as long ago as 3000 BC. Wild garlic has been around even longer. It has been found in Egyptian tombs and was believed to be an offering to the gods. It was also used in embalming oils and is still considered to be useful as a preservative. For centuries, garlic has been the number one herb for warding off vampires and bad spirits, and there are several myths and legends attached to garlic.

Today we still employ garlic in many medicinal preparations, and it's widely believed to help protect against infections, including colds and flu. It's also used to treat many infectious diseases.

GROWING ADVICE

Garlic is easy to grow and should be a part of every garden, not only for its wonderful culinary uses, but because it will also deter pests and diseases from attacking your vegetable crops. Garlic is usually grown in lines and is easier to cultivate and harvest if grown like this, but there's no reason why you couldn't scatter them in the garden. A few cloves here and there take up very little space.

Start off your crop by buying a bulb from your supermarket (choose an organic variety) or buy bulbs specially cultivated for growing from your garden supplier. Garlic specifically produced for growing will most likely give you better results, but it's possible to get a good crop from supermarket garlic bulbs.

Garlic can be planted early in the year. Prepare the ground as soon as it's workable and choose a sunny, well-drained spot in the garden. Dig over and remove any large stones, perennial weeds, and nonorganic debris. Rake to a fairly fine consistency.

Place your separated cloves, flat root end down in lines leaving about 8" (20 cm) between them. Push into the prepared soil and leave the top just slightly poking out of the ground. If you have trouble with birds, however, push them in a little more or cover with a bird-friendly netting to

Container Growing

Plant cloves in a well-drained, deep container full of fresh compost. The soil in pots and containers can dry out quickly, especially in a sunny spot, so water regularly, but don't allow pots to become waterlogged. Plant a clove or two in large pots already containing other crops. The garlic will help deter pests. Allow about 8" (20 cm) of space for each bulb to develop, then treat as you would if they were in the vegetable patch.

Garlic is very simple to grow and has many benefits, making it a garden must-have!

protect the cloves until they start to shoot. Keep the area watered, but not too wet. Generally, garlic doesn't need too much watering early in the season, but in a dry spring, check that the ground isn't drying out. Later in the summer, make sure garlic is watered regularly.

Garlic is usually immune to pests or diseases, as the strong smell deters most bugs, and its anti-bacterial properties naturally protect it from infectious diseases.

If your plants start running to seed—where they push up one strong stem and start flowering—bend the stalk down to stop the flowering process. The garlic bulbs from these plants should be used early, as they're unlikely to store very well. Many growers will simply pull up these rogue plants and use them in the kitchen straight away. There is no harm in using cloves that are green (i.e., before being left to dry), but they're usually stronger tasting.

By the end of the season, each clove will be a whole bulb. Depending on the weather through the summer months, the bulbs will mature any time from July to September. When the plants start dying back, protect them from too much rain to avoid rotting.

HARVESTING AND STORING

Let the plants die back completely and then pull up all the bulbs before the nights get too cold. Choose a sunny day and loosen the soil around each plant carefully with a fork, then gently pull

The Romans believed that garlic gave strength and workmen and soldiers were encouraged to use it. It was also supposedly a good hangover cure in Roman times.

Garlic Potatoes

A classic, fulfilling, and fairly nutritious family dish with just five ingredients and seven simple steps!

Ingredients

- 3–4 large potatoes, scrubbed or peeled and washed
- 2–3 garlic cloves (or more if preferred)
- 1–2 cups milk
- Butter, to grease dish
- ¼ cup grated cheese of your preference
- A little chopped parsley (optional, but helps sweeten the breath after eating garlic!)

Directions

1. Preheat oven to 375°F (190°C).
2. Thinly slice prepared potatoes. Boil or steam potatoes until just cooked—don't let them get too soft. Drain well and leave to cool slightly.
3. Grease a deep, oven-proof dish with the butter.
4. Crush or finely chop cloves of garlic to taste.
5. Place layers of potatoes in dish. Sprinkle garlic and chopped parsley (if using) over each layer.
6. Pour milk over the whole dish to about halfway up. Milk could be mixed with a little cream if preferred. Sprinkle with grated cheese.
7. Bake in the center of preheated oven for 15–20 minutes. Serve hot.

Note: Cheese can be added after cooking and browned off quickly under the grill if preferred.

---

them. Leave the whole plants out in the sun for a day then bring them in. Lay on racks or in boxes to dry before storing.

Garlic can be stored for many months. When the leaves are brown and dry, plait your bulbs and hang them in a cool, dark, airy place. Keep a plait hanging in the kitchen. The cloves can also be dried individually, crushed then kept in a glass jar—out of direct light—to be used as a garlic flavoring.

MEDICINAL USES FOR GARLIC

As well as being effective in preventing colds, flu, and infections, garlic is known to help reduce high blood pressure and high cholesterol. It has antifungal and antibiotic qualities.

RECIPE IDEAS

Garlic is probably the most versatile herb you can grow. Add it to everything! It will store well for months in the right conditions as well.

GINGER (*Zingiber officinale*)
(perennial)

Ginger is generally bought as a root, but in fact is a rhizome (a swelling of the underground stem). Grown in Asia since ancient times, ginger has been an important commercial crop for many centuries. It has always been used to flavor food, as well as being a useful medicinal plant.

Ginger is indigenous to tropical regions but will grow successfully in cooler climates, although it's unlikely you'll get a huge harvest in cooler regions. It needs warmth and is best grown under glass or plastic. As much as possible, imitate tropical conditions and your plants will thrive—keep them moist and warm with as much humidity as possible.

GROWING ADVICE

You can grow a ginger plant from a piece of root (rhizome) bought from a supermarket or grocer, although make sure it hasn't been treated or coated with any preservatives. Choose a piece with "eyes" that will eventually produce shoots.

Sometimes, these will be slightly raised from the rhizome and may even already have a shoot or two.

Plant the piece of rhizome with the new shoot or eye facing upwards in a large pot of rich, fresh potting compost. The pot must be well-drained since ginger will rot in waterlogged soil. Pots must be regularly watered and not allowed to dry out.

In cooler climates, ginger should be grown indoors or in a heated greenhouse, although never in direct sun. To help the plants get going, wrap the whole pot in clear plastic after watering and keep in a warm place until shoots begin to emerge.

In a warmer climate, ginger can be planted directly outside, although direct sun should be avoided. The plants should never be allowed to dry out and must be watered regularly in dry weather. Thickly mulching around your plants will keep moisture and nutrients in the soil. Heavy rainfall or over-watering could wash the nutrients out of the soil, in which case, an organic feed will help your plants thrive.

Container Growing

If your region isn't tropical or subtropical, you will need to plant ginger in containers so it can be brought indoors during cold weather. As it rarely gets hot enough in temperate climates for ginger plants to be grown outdoors, plants should probably be grown indoors year-round.

Well-drained pots or containers should be about 14" (35.5 cm) in diameter to allow space for the rhizomes to develop. Such a pot will probably be large enough for two or three plants, depending on their size. Square or oblong containers are more suitable if you intend to grow more than two or three.

HARVESTING AND STORING

When the leaves die back, ginger is ready to harvest. Fork around the plants carefully to loosen the soil before digging up. The rhizome can be used fresh and can be stored in the salad compartment of the fridge for a few days. It can also be peeled and frozen for a few months. Chop or break into pieces before freezing for convenience. Remember to label the bag or freezer container.

To dry your own ginger, follow these steps:

1. Wash and peel the root. Sometimes using a spoon is easier to peel the ginger root.
2. Slice into thin slices and lay out on a tray.
3. To dry, place tray on a sunny windowsill, use a dehydrator, or put in a very slow oven.
4. When completely dry, grind in a blender or processor until it becomes a fine powder.
5. Store in an airtight jar, label, and keep out of direct sunlight.

MEDICINAL USES FOR GINGER

In recent years, science has found that ginger has properties that aid digestion, nausea and motion sickness, and various other minor ailments. So along with its culinary delights,

Replant parts of the rhizomes you harvest and you will be getting next year's crop growing straight away.

ginger is a spice worth growing at home for its medicinal properties.

RECIPE IDEAS

Ginger can be used in many culinary preparations. It's especially good added to fruit jams or orange marmalade for extra flavor. Ginger is often preserved or candied to store it.

Ground ginger and slices of ginger root are used in many spicy recipes and can add a touch of spice and warmth to all sorts of soups and casseroles. Both Chinese and Indian cuisines use ginger root extensively—a stir-fry or a curry would be incomplete without this useful root.

Gingerbread is probably the best-known sweet recipe and usually uses ground ginger.

Gingerbread

Gingerbread doesn't have to be just for Christmas, and it really doesn't have to be shaped like a man or a star, although they are fun to make! Use any cutter you have available and try these delicious, easy-to-make gingerbread cookies.

Ingredients

- 6 tablespoons unsalted butter
- ½ cup golden syrup
- ½ cup light brown sugar
- 1¼ cup plain flour
- 2 teaspoons ground ginger
- 1 teaspoon baking soda

Directions

1. In a small pan over a low heat, stir the butter, sugar, and syrup until the sugar has dissolved. Leave to cool for 5 minutes.
2. Mix flour, ginger, and baking soda in a bowl and make a well in the center.
3. Pour in the sugar mixture and work together until a soft dough is made. Use your hands to get the best mix, but make sure the sugar mixture has cooled enough before plunging your hands in.
4. Knead the dough gently for a minute or two until smooth. Wrap in cling film and chill for 15 minutes.
5. Line two large baking tins with parchment paper. Roll out the dough to about 3 mm thick and cut out shapes. Place on baking trays, making sure they don't touch, and chill for 30 minutes.
6. While the biscuits are chilling, preheat oven to 375°F (190°C), then bake for 10 minutes. Leave to cool on the baking trays for 5 minutes, then transfer to a wire tray to cool completely.
7. If you're making gingerbread men or Christmas decorations, now's the time to get artistic and decorate with icing pens or your own cake decorating method!

HORSERADISH (*Cochlearia armoracia*)
(perennial)

Horseradish has been traced back to around 1500 BC. The ancient Greeks used it as a liniment, and it was also thought to have aphrodisiac powers. Over the centuries, horseradish has been described as being worth its weight in gold and been used to treat everything from rheumatism to chest and lung disease.

It is believed to have originated in central Europe and eventually spread to all parts of Europe and North America. As it became established as an herb that had beneficial constituents, as well as being nourishing and easy on the palate, horseradish became widely used and commercialized. It's a prolific growing plant and will become invasive in a garden if not checked.

GROWING ADVICE

Horseradish should be positioned carefully in the garden. To inhibit rapid spreading, containers work well, as they literally contain the plant. It will tolerate partial shade, but prefers a sunny spot.

Choose a permanent place in the garden carefully and wisely, as horseradish will last many years.

Dig the ground deep and clear out any weeds, large stones, and nonorganic debris. The cleaner the soil, the bigger the roots will grow. More preparation will guarantee better crops. The horseradish root likes a rich, well-manured soil that's not too heavy. All root crops struggle in heavy soils.

Horseradish is usually grown from root cuttings, which you can buy from garden suppliers. Plant the root in early spring or autumn. Check the supplier's growing recommendations, as the size of the root, the variety, and region will have varying needs.

A neighbor or local gardener may be happy to donate a root or two to start you off. Plant as soon as possible after the roots have been lifted from the soil. Plant the roots according to how big they are; the smaller the root, the shallower it should be planted. Try taking your own root cuttings in the autumn. Dig the roots up gently and use the

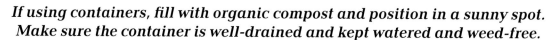

If using containers, fill with organic compost and position in a sunny spot. Make sure the container is well-drained and kept watered and weed-free.

largest one in the kitchen, then replant one or more of the side shoots.

Also, sections of root can be planted in the spring to produce new roots in the autumn. Horseradish does spread quickly, though, and care should be taken to not let it overrun the whole garden. For container growing, choose a large, well-drained container and fill with fresh compost before planting.

From Seed

Horseradish can be grown from seed sown in spring. The seeds should be sown in a sunny patch and the ground must be cleaned of large stones and perennial weeds and dug deeply before sowing to allow for root growth. Again, the cleaner and richer the soil, the better chance you have of harvesting a good crop. Thin out

Container Growing

If you have limited space for growing your herbs, spices, and vegetable crops, growing horseradish in containers may be more practical. Horseradish roots tend to be invasive if left to their own devices and it's easy to miss one or two when digging up in the autumn. Use deep containers; as with all root crops, horseradish needs a good depth of soil. Always use fresh compost every year to ensure the soil is full of the nutrients required to develop the roots of your plants. Don't let them dry out, but always make sure the containers are well-drained, as horseradish won't tolerate being waterlogged.

A horseradish plant in the garden.

the plants when they're about 2" (5 cm) high to allow space to grow. Keep weed-free and watered especially during dry periods.

Alternatively, sow seed in a large, well-drained container. Always use fresh compost when planting containers, as old compost may have been drained of nutrients from previous plantings.

Once established, and with very little attention, the horseradish patch will become permanent and will produce healthy roots for many years. Dig up all the roots every autumn. Use the largest roots in the kitchen and replant the others. This method of cultivation keeps your horseradish patch producing roots regularly and controls the rapid growth.

Homemade Horseradish Sauce

Keep in mind that fresh horseradish is very strong; add other ingredients with this in mind.
For example, Dijon mustard has a milder taste. Make it to your own preference.

Ingredients
- Horseradish root
- ½ cup sour or heavy cream
- Pinch of mustard powder, or 1 teaspoon Dijon mustard
- 1 tablespoon white wine vinegar

Optional ingredients/extras:
- 1 tablespoon finely chopped chives
- 1 tablespoon mayonnaise
- Salt and pepper, to taste

Directions
1. Prepare the horseradish by washing, peeling, and finely grating the root. You want to end up with about 1 tablespoon of grated root. Soak in a small amount of hot water for 10 minutes to soften slightly. Drain well.
2. Mix prepared root with all other ingredients. Blend or mix well. Taste, adding more seasoning if needed.
3. Chill for 30 minutes before serving.

HARVESTING AND STORING

Horseradish root is said to be stronger tasting after the first frost, so if you can leave them in until then, you will get a better result.

Store cleaned roots in a paper bag for up to a week in the fridge. After that, the taste will diminish and they will start to shrivel. Smaller roots can be stored in sand for planting out in the spring. The best way to store horseradish is to make a sauce and seal in airtight glass jars. Leaves should be used fresh.

MEDICINAL USES FOR HORSERADISH

Horseradish root can be made into a syrup to ease bronchitis, coughs, and colds. The sliced raw root is also said to be effective in treating boils and infected wounds.

Large doses can cause sickness and horseradish remedies aren't advisable for people with stomach ulcers or thyroid problems.

RECIPE IDEAS

Horseradish root is commonly used as an accompaniment to fish and meat dishes. The root is grated and eaten raw. The young leaves are tasty and are suitable for adding to salads or in sandwiches.

Take a few from each plant and allow to grow again before using more. The root is cleaned, grated, and eaten raw, often mixed with vinegar and cream and served with a Sunday roast.

MUSTARD (*Sinapis alba*)
(annual)

Although mustard is a very hot-tasting spice, it doesn't need a hot climate in order to grow. Acres of mustard have been grown commercially in Europe for a very long time, certainly since the sixteenth century.

English and French mustards are sold all over the world in slightly different recipe forms. In the early eighteenth century, it was discovered that adding water to the fine, crushed, and powdered seeds of mustard produced the very hot flavor associated with mustard. However, if the ground mustard seed is mixed with milk or cream, you get a milder taste. Some French mustards have whole grains left in and with various other ingredients, create a very different taste to the traditionally hot English mustard.

Mustard leaves are edible and can be used as a vegetable, adding flavor to many dishes, but as the seed is generally considered to have the true mustard taste, mustard is nearly always thought of as a spice. Over the years, many countries have developed their own mustard recipes, and each will have their own distinguishing flavors, consistencies, and even colors.

GROWING ADVICE

Mustard grows very successfully in temperate regions because it prefers a cooler climate. Seed can be sown early in the spring in most regions. White mustard is an easy crop to grow and will come up on its own year after year in an ideal environment.

Seed should be sown directly outside in a well-drained sunny spot. Prepare the soil by digging over and removing any perennial weeds and large stones, then hoe or rake over to a fine consistency. The finer the topsoil, the easier the seeds will germinate and put down roots.

Sow in rows about ¼–½" (0.5–1 cm) deep and leave about 9–12" (23–30.5 cm) between rows.

Micro greens can be ready to eat in just a few days.

Container Growing

There doesn't appear to be any good reason why mustard plants can't be grown in containers, however, plants can grow up to 3' (91 cm) tall, so the pots or containers will need to be fairly large and may need supporting canes. Canes should be placed before planting to avoid damaging roots.

Keep in a sunny spot, but don't keep indoors as mustard prefers a cooler temperature. The pots should be well-drained, but never allowed to dry out. Use fresh compost to get the most from your plants, although generally mustard seed will do well in most garden soils. Check your seed packet for any other growing recommendations for your region or variety.

Or grow your mustard seeds as micro greens in small containers. Containers should be well-drained, and compost kept watered. Sow seeds and keep in a dark, warm place. Seeds should germinate in two or three days. Mist with water and keep warm and dark until plants are a couple of inches tall.

Sow as thinly as possible by placing one seed every few inches. This will mean less thinning out when the seedlings have started to grow. Water regularly, especially in dry weather, and keep free from weeds. Weeds will take nutrients from the soil and leave less for your plants to feed on. Mustard takes only a couple of months from germination to harvesting, so it's possible to sow lines of seed every few weeks to have a constant supply. However, this does take up valuable space in the garden. Mustard is a good early crop to grow, and once harvested, the space can be used for heat-loving crops in the summer months.

HARVESTING AND STORING
To harvest the seed, the plants should be left until the last possible moment. Use the leaves sparingly as the plants start to develop. Only take one or two from each plant at a time, and allow them to regrow before picking again. Pods of seeds pop open when ripe and spray the seeds around, so to

Homemade Mustard Sauce

A classic kitchen staple, make your own mustard with this delicious recipe!

Ingredients

- ½ cup mustard seeds
- 1¼ cups white wine (or you can use beer or vinegar instead)
- Seasoning of your preference

Directions

1. Soak seeds in wine for 12–24 hours. The seeds will soften and have absorbed much of the wine.
2. Strain, reserving liquid.
3. Grind the seeds to a paste using a mortar and pestle, a small blender, or a food processor.
4. Add reserved liquid to paste slowly to achieve the consistency you want.
5. Sieve if you want a very smooth result.
6. Taste and add seasoning if preferred. Honey, salt, pepper, sugar, or finely chopped fresh herbs could be added according to your taste. A little ground turmeric or marigold petals will add color and flavor.

save missing it, place a cloth or piece of cardboard around the plants to catch them. Otherwise, pick pods and dry off for a day in the sun or in a bright, airy spot. Pick the pods as the plant starts to lose its color and is dying back.

Mustard seed will last for a year or more when kept in jars and stored out of direct light. After harvesting the pods, spread seeds out on a tray in a bright place for a few hours to dry before storing. Mustard condiments can be made at home using simple recipes. Mustard greens are best used on the day they are picked.

MEDICINAL USES FOR MUSTARD

Mustard poultices have been used for centuries. At one time, mustard was known as the "singer's herb" because of its success in treating sore throats. Breathing in the vapor of boiling water poured over mustard seeds can help fight off colds and coughs.

RECIPE IDEAS

Mustard greens can be added to almost any soup, casserole, or stir fry. Add near the end of cooking, as mustard greens only need to be wilted like spinach. The leaves have a spicy taste and are usually less bitter than kale or other brassicas.

The most common use of mustard is as a condiment in the form of a sauce and can be served with most meat dishes. Mix a spoonful of mustard sauce into beaten eggs before scrambling to liven the eggs up.

POPPIES (*Papaver somniferum*)
(annual)

Although freshly baked poppy seed bread is irresistible, poppies are, in fact, illegal to cultivate in some countries and regions. Check with the legislation locally before you sow poppy seeds in your garden. When the flower has finished blooming, the opium poppy produces a latex in the seed pod that is commonly known as opium and is further processed into the drug heroin. The obvious dangers of heroin are the reason why poppies aren't always legal to grow.

Over many parts of the world, poppies grow wild and are an attractive meadow flower, often found in packets of mixed wildflower or meadow seeds. Other varieties don't produce the same opiate as the opium poppy. They're an annual plant, but will often reseed themselves in ideal conditions.

Although poppy flowers appear delicate, the plants are quite resilient. The discovery of a bright red field of poppies in Flanders during World War I gave rise to the poppy being a symbol of courage and poppies are worn on Remembrance Day every year in the UK.

GROWING ADVICE

Seed should be sown *in situ*, as poppies don't like to be replanted. Choose a sunny, well-drained spot in the flower garden or use as a border or edging plant. And, if possible, keep out of windy spots—the plants have a delicate stem and can be blown over in a gust of wind. Dig over the ground and prepare by removing all perennial weeds and large stones, then rake or hoe the soil to a fine consistency. As with all seeds planted directly outside, they will have a better chance of germination if the soil is fine and well prepared beforehand.

Sow seed thinly, as seedlings will need thinning out later on. Check the seed packet for regional variations in sowing times. Poppy seed can

The flowers of the red poppy are sometimes used to color wines and other products. However, all parts of the poppy, apart from the ripe seeds, are dangerous to consume.

Poppy seeds are versatile in the kitchen and are worth cultivating and collecting.

often be sown in spring or autumn, but regional differences should be checked first. Lightly cover the seeds with soil and gently water with a fine spray or rosette attachment on a watering can. Make sure the seeds are covered after watering. If the ground doesn't completely dry out, seed should germinate fairly quickly. Never over-water, though. When seedlings are a few inches high, they should be thinned to about 1" (2.5 cm) apart.

Keep weeds away to avoid nutrients being drawn from the soil. Weeds and other plants can also strangle the roots of young poppy plants. Protect from wind and heavy rain if plants are isolated. In a wildflower meadow environment, poppies tend to hold their own and be supported by other wildflowers, but in a garden, they may need a little looking after. The beautiful flowers, and the later culinary seeds, make it worthwhile! When the plants have finished flowering, they produce a seed capsule that should be left as long as possible for the seeds inside to ripen. Gently tap the pod from time to time, and you will hear or feel the seeds rattling inside.

HARVESTING AND STORING

Leave the pods on the plant to reseed if they have had a successful year. However, if a very cold winter is expected, or the flowers weren't as healthy as they could've been, collect the seed by removing pods when the seeds are ripe and try another location next year if you want them to reseed.

Plants that have been grown from hybrids will revert back to the original wild varieties—either *Papaver somniferous* (opium poppy) or *Papaver rhoeas* (corn or field poppy)—when left to reseed themselves. Hybrid varieties will need sowing every year to prevent this from happening.

Container Growing

Poppies can be grown in containers, although they're originally a field crop and will probably do better in open ground. However, new hybrid varieties of *Papaver somniferum* may be more suitable for container growing. Always make sure your containers or pots are well-drained and don't allow them to completely dry out.

The "wild" or original varieties of poppy tend to grow to over 12" (30.5 cm) high, so they should be placed behind lower-growing plants to avoid overshadowing in a cramped space, such as a window box or other container.

Poppy Seed Pound Cake

Sweet, buttery, and delicious, this pound cake is sure to be a new favorite!

Ingredients

- 1 cup unsalted butter, softened
- 1 cup sugar
- 1 cup self-rising flour
- 1–2 teaspoons baking powder
- 3 eggs, beaten
- 3 tablespoons whole milk
- 1 teaspoon vanilla extract
- 2 tablespoons poppy seeds
- Thin slices of orange (optional)

Directions

1. Preheat oven to 350°F (177°C).
2. Line a loaf tin with parchment paper.
3. Put all ingredients, except for the poppy seeds, into a large bowl and mix with an electric whisk or a wooden spoon until smooth.
4. Stir in the poppy seeds and mix well.
5. Pour mixture into prepared tin, spread evenly, and bake for 40–45 minutes.
6. Top with sliced oranges during the last 10–15 minutes of cooking, if using.
7. Cool on a wire tray.

Poppy seed can be collected and stored as soon as it is ripe and kept in labelled jars out of direct light.

MEDICINAL USES FOR POPPIES

Although the latex can be processed to make heroin, it's also processed into a pure morphine and has been used as a medical pain-relieving drug for many years.

RECIPE IDEAS

Poppy seed doesn't contain any opium or other adverse ingredients, so whole seeds can be added safely to homemade breads, soups, curries, chutneys, and other recipes. Seeds can be crushed and mixed with other ground spices. Poppy seed oil is processed for culinary use and an artist's oil.

SAFFRON (*Crocus sativus*)
(annual)

Saffron, at the time of writing, is probably the most expensive spice known to mankind. It takes around 150,000 flowers and hundreds of hours of labor to produce a couple of pounds of dried saffron threads. Only a small amount is used at a time, though, so this is a good reason to grow it yourself.

Saffron spice comes from the stigmas or fronds of the flower *Crocus sativus* and is believed to originate in India. In recent years, it has spread over many regions and is cultivated in Europe, as well as Middle Eastern countries. Saffron has been one of the most revered herbs for thousands of years and was cultivated for use as early as the eleventh century.

GROWING ADVICE

Although saffron is a hardy plant and will survive in cooler climates, it may not flower in poor summers. A greenhouse or bright conservatory may be a better spot if you're in a region where summer sunshine is not very reliable.

Plants are propagated from "corms," which resemble bulbs and in ideal conditions, will multiply every year. They can be left in the ground for three or four years, sometimes longer before they need to be dug up and separated.

Prepare a very sunny well-drained spot in the garden. Saffron likes rich soil, so it's a good idea to dig in some well-rotted compost during the season before planting. Dig over the soil and remove any perennial weeds and large stones. Rake or hoe to a fine consistency. Corms should be planted in mid-summer to flower the following year.

Buy corms from a reliable supplier and be sure to get the right variety—only *Crocus sativus* produces saffron. **All other crocus varieties are**

inedible. Sometimes larger corms planted earlier in the summer will flower in the same year as planting, but generally, a year should be allowed before plants flower. Plant soon after buying, as the corms will be healthier the fresher they are.

Only a small amount of saffron will be available from each flower, so plant a whole line if possible. Dig a hole that's about 4" (10 cm) deep for each corm and allow about 4" (10 cm) between each one. Check on the growing recommendations on the packet for any variations for your region. Let the soil dry out during the summer, but water from time to time in late summer or autumn when

Each saffron plant (or "mother") produces about three to four "daughter" corms.

Container Growing

The saffron crocus will grow well in containers or large pots. Make sure pots are well-drained and filled with rich, fresh compost. In regions with shorter or unreliable summers, container growing may be the best way to achieve good results.

Position in the sunniest, warmest spot in the garden or in a conservatory or greenhouse. The flowers need a lot of sun to develop, so gently move containers around during the day to catch the sun.

Plant corms as you would in the garden and allow enough space for each plant to grow. They may need repotting every year in fresh compost to keep the corms healthy and producing enough flowers.

the flowers start appearing. Leaves will grow taller than the flower stem and will stay green for many months after the plants have finished flowering. Leave them to die back naturally.

If a very cold winter is expected, gently dig up the corms and plant in a container for the winter or keep them in a plastic bag with a little compost and store in a dark, cool place in the house before planting out again when the weather warms up. They can also be protected with mulch or even a plastic cloche.

HARVESTING AND STORING

Whole flowers can be collected just before opening and stigmas removed afterwards, or, if the sun has been kind and the flowers are blooming, collect the stigmas directly from the flowers while still on the plants. Harvest saffron by pulling the stigmas from the center of the flowers. Lay the saffron threads carefully on a tray and dry very slowly in a cool oven, or in the sun, if possible, until completely dry. Store in an airtight jar out of direct light.

Saffron Rice

Another way to change up rice, this recipe is another delicious alternative.

Ingredients

- ¾ cup basmati rice (for 2 servings)
- ¼ cup hot water
- 3¼ cups chicken or golden vegetable stock
- ½–¾ cup minced yellow or white onion
- 2 tablespoons olive oil
- ¾ teaspoon salt
- ¼ teaspoon saffron threads

Directions

1. Put half the saffron threads into a mortar and grind to a powder with a pestle.
2. Add the rest of the saffron threads to the mortar. Don't crush them. Add the hot water and leave it to soak for 5 minutes to open up the taste.
3. Rinse rice in a strainer until water runs clear.
4. Heat the oil in a large, heavy-based saucepan and add the onion. Cook gently for a few minutes until soft, stirring to avoid sticking, for about 10 minutes.
5. Add rice to the pan. Stir the onion in and gently sauté for another minute or two.
6. Pour over the saffron liquid and the stock and stir.
7. Bring to a boil, stir, and boil for about half a minute.
8. Cover the pan with lid and reduce heat. Simmer for about 20 minutes.
9. Remove from heat and let the rice steam by itself for another 10 minutes. Leave the lid on the pan.
10. Fluff up with a fork before serving.

MEDICINAL USES FOR SAFFRON

Saffron was used as a digestive aid and as a mild sedative in days gone past. However, high doses of saffron have shown to be detrimental to health and today it's not commonly used as a medicinal spice.

RECIPE IDEAS

Saffron has a distinctive honey/bitter taste and will color and flavor food well. Threads can be soaked in hot water for a while to release the flavor or crumbled and added directly to the cooking pot.

To turn dried threads into powder, grind with a mortar and pestle or the back of a teaspoon.

Cooking Conversion Chart

WEIGHT

IMPERIAL	METRIC
1/2 oz	15 g
1 oz	29 g
2 oz	57 g
3 oz	85 g
4 oz	113 g
5 oz	141 g
6 oz	170 g
8 oz	227 g
10 oz	283 g
12 oz	340 g
13 oz	369 g
14 oz	397 g
15 oz	425 g
1 lb	453 g

MEASUREMENT

CUP	ONCES	MILLILITERS	TABLESPOONS
8 cup	64 oz	1895 ml	128
6 cup	48 oz	1420 ml	96
5 cup	40 oz	1180 ml	80
4 cup	32 oz	960 ml	64
2 cup	16 oz	480 ml	32
1 cup	8 oz	240 ml	16
3/4 cup	6 oz	177 ml	12
2/3 cup	5 oz	158 ml	11
1/2 cup	4 oz	118 ml	8
3/8 cup	3 oz	90 ml	6
1/3 cup	2.5 oz	79 ml	5.5
1/4 cup	2 oz	59 ml	4
1/8 cup	1 oz	30 ml	3
1/16 cup	1/2 oz	15 ml	1

TEMPERATURE

FARENHEIT	CELSIUS
100 °F	37 °C
150 °F	65 °C
200 °F	93 °C
250 °F	121 °C
300 °F	150 °C
325 °F	160 °C
350 °F	180 °C
375 °F	190 °C
400 °F	200 °C
425 °F	220 °C
450 °F	230 °C
500 °F	260 °C
525 °F	274 °C
550 °F	288 °C

Further Reading

Growing Winter Food by Linda Gray

Useful Websites

https://botanical.com/
https://www.rhs.org.uk/
https://healthylivingbooks.org/

Photography Credits

Index

Note: Page numbers in *italics* indicate recipes.

About the Author

Linda Gray is a home and garden expert from London, England. She spent two years traveling with her partner and four children before settling on an acre of land in rural France. In spite of her city background, she created a garden that produced enough food to feed her family practically every day of the year.

For more than ten years, she and her family were nourished with organic herbs, fruits, and vegetables, and enjoyed healthy lives with no need for antibiotics.

Inspired to share her experiences, Linda started writing and has published many books and guides on healthy living.

She regularly writes blogs and articles to help readers live a happier and healthier lifestyle on her website, www.healthylivingbooks.org, where all of her books are also listed.